Why French Children Don't Talk Back

Catherine Crawford

JOHN MURRAY

First published in Great Britain in 2012 by John Murray (Publishers)
An Hachette UK Company

First published in paperback in 2013

1

Lines from *Super Nanny* used by permission of Hachette Pratique.

A CIP catalogue record for this title is available from the British Library

ISBN 978-1-84854-714-8

Typeset by Hewer Text UK Ltd, Edinburgh
Printed and bound by Clays Ltd, St Ives plc

John Murray policy is to use papers that are natural, renewable and recyclable
products and made from wood grown in sustainable forests. The logging and
manufacturing processes are expected to conform to the environmental
regulations of the country of origin.

John Murray (Publishers)
338 Euston Road
London NW1 3BH

www.johnmurray.co.uk

For my surprisingly French, indefatigable parents,
Dorothy and Bill Crawford

'œuf means egg . . . chapeau means hat . . .
it's like . . . those French . . . have a
different word, for everything!'

STEVE MARTIN

Contents

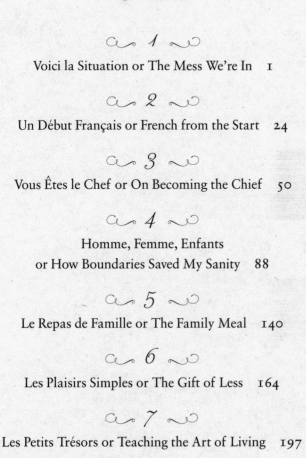

I

Voici la Situation or The Mess We're In

As a mother with two young daughters in a trendy, urban neighbourhood hedged in by hordes of other trendy, urban families, I often feel a keen sense of bafflement at what I see going on with the procreators in my midst. At the risk of being a traitor to my generation, I have to say: I don't know when or how it happened, but it's clear to me that even as we have tried harder than any of our ancestors to mentor, please and encourage our kids, we have completely lost control of them, and in the process we've lost control of our own lives as well. And it isn't pretty. How ugly is it? Three words: baby yoga pants.

I live in Park Slope, Brooklyn, quite possibly the world headquarters of helicopter parents, but I've seen similar abdication in Manhattan, Portland, Oregon, San Francisco, Seattle and Los Angeles. These are just the cities I visit regularly; I have a pretty good hunch it's happening in nearly every middle-class neighbourhood in the USA,

Canada and the UK. (How can I be so sure? Here are just a couple of the many ways: I'd be willing to wager that you know (all too well?) a parent who lives in fear of their toddler, or that you're aware that a Bugaboo is not merely a synonym for a hobgoblin.) My sources in London report that Clapham (Nappy Valley), Primrose Hill and Highgate are particularly afflicted.

I have absolute *certainty* that some thirty-odd years ago my mother didn't pick me up from school laden with four snack choices to ensure my satisfaction (and avoid a meltdown), and that she didn't put in a lot of time worrying that she wasn't being the best mother she could possibly be. But nowadays these are the types of thoughts that pack the days of every parent I know. I count myself very much among them (sorry, Ma!). I'm ready for change.

Although the familiar dictum 'children should be seen, not heard' may be a bit harsh – and the truth is, I enjoy hearing my kids much of the time – I'm afraid that the new trend of seeing, hearing, pondering, analyzing, cogitating, working through, and giving in to our children is no better. And it may even be worse: new research suggests that kids who are too often encouraged to share every last scrap of a thought, and then praised for whatever they share, tend to suffer later in life when teachers, bosses and other mentor figures are less inclined to adore each effort.

I love my kids dearly, but sometimes I honestly couldn't care less how they feel after a harmless skirmish in the playground or what their concerns are when they do something wrong and are punished. I yearn (but have yet) to steal the phrase my dad employed often during my own upbringing: 'I don't care what you think! I'll do the thinking for all of us!'

About seven years ago, when I was new to the mothering game, I'd watch parents in the same overwhelmed boat as me with the hope that I'd learn secrets to child-rearing in this exciting, challenging and liberated age: *Ahh, that mother is now massaging her son who just threw sand in the eyes of a baby. Was he just too tense? That's why he acted up?* Note to self: *keep baby relaxed.* In my neighbourhood, I see a lot of 'talking it out'. It is not uncommon to overhear parents encourage their children to express their feelings while, say, in restaurants:

'Why do you want to jump on the table, Liam?'
'Coco, please try to explain your anger towards the green beans.'

There's a mindset in these parts that children should be treated like adults, with all of their tastes and dislikes respected.

Growing up with twelve siblings and roughly zero of my tastes and dislikes even acknowledged, the word 'respect' was generally only uttered in the context of what the small residents of the house should have for the taller inhabitants; this sounded OK to me. After all, kids are people too – short, and often totally unreasonable people – but people none the less. In practice, however, this notion was a lot less quaint.

I remember my older daughter Oona, two years old at

the time, telling me that my 'words were hurting' her. My grievous offence? I'd asked her to bring me her shoes. I also remember thinking – a little to my horror – 'Oh, I'll show you something that hurts.' Thankfully, I only laughed and left the room, leaving her utterly outraged. But early on, I had my doubts about this new sort of level playing field between parent and child. After all, until about seven or eight years of age (if you are lucky) kids are, by nature, irrational.

My suspicions were realized one evening when my French friend, Lucie, came to dinner with her husband and two children. The Durand kids were obedient, respectful and, when told to be, actually quiet. They didn't seem to require cajoling or lengthy explanations when asked to set the table. They simply did what they were told. If they didn't want a certain dish at dinner, they didn't eat it, but they also were not offered a myriad of other choices. Not a single cheese stick was proffered.

After dinner we parents were sitting around the dining room table finishing a bottle of wine while the kids played in the living room. *A mother could get used to this*, I thought, reclining – yes, reclining! – in my chair. But the sweet, slightly inebriated reverie did not last long.

Soon enough, my younger daughter, Daphne, wanted my attention, so she did what she usually does – namely, she started going bananas, screaming and yelling for me. (This was back when Daph would dive to the ground at the slightest provocation in order to better express her tantrums, pounding and kicking the floor with such exuberance that we referred to this move as 'pulling a

McEnroe'; more on this later. But, for clarification, I'm referring of course to John McEnroe, the American tennis *enfant terrible*. Think also in terms of the former French international footballer Nicolas 'Le Sulk' Anelka and the English footballer Joey Barton.)

By this point I'd been exposed to the well-oiled Durand machine for about four hours, more than enough time to soak up some deep wisdom. So, instead of doing what I usually do – tending immediately to Daphne's (loud) calls – I looked to Lucie for advice. Here, I should note, Lucie and her husband both appeared blissfully unaware of the three-foot raving maniac in the other room. Perhaps it was the wine? *Mais, non*!

Lucie must have sensed my hunger for advice, for now she was leaning across the table, putting a strong, steady hand on my arm, and offering an adage she told me her Parisian mother had often employed: 'If there's no blood, don't get up.'

If there is no blood, don't get up.

So simple – and excellent. Of course!

That is how they do it. No blood, no foul! Parenting as a basketball – or football – game.

So I didn't get up. Things were loud for a little bit, and Daphne was irate with my lack of bustle on her behalf. And then, as fast as her wails had started, they stopped and she resumed playing with the other kids.

After that night I began watching my friend very closely for additional clues on how she handled her children. For a while I thought I was just being charmed by that thing that always gets me – little kids fluent in French. I mean, how cute is that! Maybe, in their perfect French, they were telling their mother to eat *merde* and die. But I knew that wasn't the case. There was no eye-rolling, no door slamming, stomping, banging on walls, floors or ceilings, no food throwing, no pleading – you get the picture. In fact, there didn't appear to be a whole lot of resistance at all to the words coming down from on high. That is, from Mum and Dad. Unfortunately, my French is *très* rusty and I missed much of the invaluable wisdom to be gathered like precious parenting stones when Lucie spoke with her children. Still, I was convinced that there was very little negotiating or backtalk going on. When I cornered Lucie later – cornered her gently, politely, that is, albeit perhaps in a slightly wild-eyed frenzy because of my sleep-deprived desperation – she confirmed that this was the case.

Soon, whenever things spun out of control in my own home, I found myself wondering: What would Lucie Durand do? Swallowing my pride, along with plenty of the kids' uneaten dinners, I took things a bit further and started asking her, point blank, for advice. For instance, when Daphne decorated the length of our rather long hallway with crayon (*oh, McEnroe*), my husband and I were unsure how to react. Most of the parenting books we owned cautioned against drawing too much attention to a specific incident when disciplining a child. The theory is that if you make a big fuss over a single act, the child will remember its effects and likely repeat the offence for a moment in the spotlight at a later date. Next time, we feared, Daphne might paint the whole apartment!

We didn't know what to do with her. Time out? Stern warning? Daph was just shy of three years old, so taking away privileges or toys wouldn't really register much with her. When I asked Lucie what they might do in France with this type of toddler misdemeanour, she didn't hesitate: 'You go to the kitchen and get a sponge with soap and water. Sit her on a stool and have her scrub.' I was incredulous: scrub it all off? My husband tried this himself and couldn't erase so much as a single scrawl. Then Lucie assured me that I only needed to make Daphne wash the wall for a minute so that she had a chance to understand the consequences of her action – and to see how damn hard it is to get crayon off a wall.

It seemed so obvious. Yet somehow, in the hyper-attentive, must-do-the-right-thing parenting environment in which I'd been marinating, nothing was obvious any more. For her part, Lucie is always flattered and happy to help, but she was also a bit baffled by my lack of know-how. An expert parent she is, yes, but Lucie is not a parenting expert. Her approach to childrearing, in her mind, is neither groundbreaking nor new; it's simply the way things are done in her homeland. Often Lucie has a strategy or phrase that does wonders for any given stand-off between me and my kids, but more than that, it's her refreshing attitude: there shouldn't be any stand-offs. 'After all, Catherine,' she often reminds me, 'you are the Chief.'

The Chief – it has a nice ring to it, yes?

For me, Lucie is a goldmine of great advice, but she's made it very clear that hers is the natural way that practically everyone parents in France. Here in the States we've been talking and talking and talking about our kids' feelings. Meanwhile, over there *French children don't talk back*!

It was around this time that I had a major Frenchified epiphany: I could become the Chief of my family, with my husband as able-bodied second-in-command, and together we could reclaim from the children control of the household, the playground, the supermarket and more. Our lives! We could have our pre-kid lives back to some extent. Actually this would be an improved version of that past life. Because, to paraphrase that surprisingly French, filthily hilarious comedian Louis C. K.: I love my children more than anything in the world, and sometimes I wish they had never been born. Most parents I know, if they are being completely honest, would say the same thing. Put another, more French, way, we all very much want to spend time with our children and to do everything we can – within reason – to help them have happy, successful lives. But boy, oh boy, sometimes we just want to be left alone for five minutes – or five days.

More than that, we need this time. The paradox I've observed in the playgrounds of several American cities is that even as we work ourselves to dust to ensure that our kids are thrilled beyond a shadow of a sliver of a doubt, we the parents are suffering in the process. Exhausted, dissatisfied parents can't be good for the kids – in any country. I've certainly felt myself get sucked into this nasty cycle – contorting every which way to please the kids, only to resent them for making my life so hard.

That is why, with the help of many a wise French parent, I finally decided to do something about it, and brought my whole family on a bit of an adventure.

And, no, I didn't consult Oona and Daphne for their thoughts on the matter. So let me now say to my two, sweet, unbelievably wonderful and interesting girls who will one day read this book: I'm sorry. Am I sorry for trying to make all our lives easier, simpler, more satisfying, and more deeply felt? Not at all. But I am sorry you didn't have a say in being part of this great and ambitious effort. (The truth is that, even early on, it was not uncommon for one or both kids to plead with me as I slipped into Chief mode: 'But *Moooooooom*. We. Are. Not. French!') I am sorry for making you the main characters in a narrative you had no chance to approve. Luckily, you are both great kids, so I don't think you will ever be too embarrassed by your portrayal.

Phew, glad that's done! Now, here goes. Like most children, our kids were very young when the personalities we see solidifying several years on began to form. They were both still babies really when my husband, Mac, developed a shorthand for describing the girls to friends and family members who asked after them: Oona was the Pulitzer Prize-winning novelist Edith Wharton; Daphne was John Belushi. John Belushi, for those not familiar with him, was a beloved American comic maniac revered as much for his brilliance as for his lack of self-control. If his name doesn't ring a bell, you can think of Daphne as a cross between the comedians Jack Black and Lucille Ball. Or, go with another more recent nickname that's stuck to Daphne: 'the Courtney Love of Kindergarten'. To explain further, Daphne's McEnroe moments were only when she excelled in the tantrum-throwing arts. What this means is that Oona has always been contemplative about life – a keen observer, a big feeler, a bigger thinker and, dare I say, oddly introspective for a child. She wrote her first book at three. She started her first blog – reviewing books she liked – at seven. Oona is the kind of kid who will hang out with teachers at school dances. There was even a period when she wrote stories in bed. Hence Edith Wharton.

Daphers' is another, wilder story. The kid, bless her spazzy heart, has one speed – and it is not slow. She falls asleep twitching with energy – and for many years did not fall asleep for many hours – and wakes up barrelling into our bed. At 7 a.m. – or earlier. No matter when she goes to bed. There is a chance that Daphne is a marvel of science: she can crash out at midnight and rise at 6.30 ready for a pro wrestling match – or at least a round of not very delicate grappling with her dad. She is bouncy and grabby and loud – and always has been. She will start her share of food fights in life. She's a Belushi.

That wrestling match with her dad, by the way, is one she wins, because my husband himself is more Wharton than Belushi. Mac is a slow waker who can pound a double espresso after dinner and sleep like a baby that night (provided the baby in question is not Daphne).

So where does Daph get it from? Well, let's see – if Oona is like Mac, then . . . yep, Daphne is me. As a kid I fought back with limb-flailing freak-outs as my nine

– nine! – brothers routinely held me down and farted in my face while calling me 'Cat Urine'. In my youth soccer pictures, I was the kid with scabs on my chin. As a pre-teen, I preferred roller skates to sneakers.

Being a Belushi means, of course, much more than operating at a one-speed frenzy. It also means Daphne is hilarious. Daphne might just, in fact, be a comic genius. From a very early age, she was capable of cracking us up with her physical comedy – is it possible a two-year-old knows what a pratfall is?

As befitting her nickname, Oona's humour is more cerebral than Daph's. Recently, she's taken to telling a 'Joke of the Day'. An example: 'Why did the elephant paint her nails red? So she could hide in a cherry tree.'

As the girls grow older, the Wharton–Belushi dynamic has blurred a little, but it remains mostly intact. For a parent, each type presents unique challenges. Edith Wharton children think they are smarter than their parents (and while this may be true, that is beside the point), so eye-rolling insolence begins at a shockingly early age. As sharp observers of humanity, Whartons may see much that is unsavoury – the world is, naturally, populated with smokers and litterers – and be tempted to correct, or at least point out, such behaviour. It can be challenging to remind Whartons that adults must be respected if possible and that they will likely not respond well to receiving admonishments from a waist-high whistle-blower.

The John Belushi child, as we've seen, is prone to unhesi-tatingly prostrate performances of unhappiness. (When

Belushis morph into McEnroes.) Their indoor voices are a fine volume, so long as the indoors you are talking about is a shopping mall or a domed stadium. Belushis can have a tenuous relationship with truth. Part of this is because they like to see how much they can get away with. I don't mean this in the piles of cocaine sense of the taxonomy's namesake, but still a parent can't help wondering if a sneaked second slice of cake is a gateway dessert.

And so: Oona and Daphne – Wharton and Belushi – thank you for being my favourite two kids in the whole world and for helping me Frenchify our existence. Counting Mac, I could not have asked for three better partners on this very important project to see if French parenting techniques can translate to my life.

Even the littlest among us – Daphers – ultimately took to the new style with surprising dedication, if not great enthusiasm. One morning she woke up – at 7 a.m. on the dot – and, still bleary-eyed, said: 'I wonder what French throw-up looks like.'

Yes, it seems we'd all become fairly obsessed with how things are done over there. That's not to say all French kids are perfectly behaved master oil painters and, conversely, all American kids are materialistic brats or can be represented by those holy terrors on the television programme *Toddlers and Tiaras*. I am only saying that we Yanks, and our not so distant Brit cousins, could do with reconsidering our parenting approach, and the French mothers I know certainly provide an excellent example of how we might improve our lives – and, by extension, our kids' lives.

Curiously, it was not only Oona and Daphne's response that surprised me as I set out to Frenchify our existence, I was also thrown a curve by the reactions of fellow parents in the same situation. In the 'Raw Nerves Hall of Fame' there should be a special wing for parents. Everywhere I turned, from within my own family to the benches at the playground, I encountered serious resistance to my ideas and undertaking – even when I counted myself among the most needy of a little parenting tune-up. Moms don't like to be wrong or second-guessed. Now that I think back on my own mother's childrearing style, I suppose that should not have been much of a surprise. When it comes to their children, people's feelings are very sensitive. Rightly so. We love those little maniacs to pieces. Believe me when I say that this is not an attack on American parents. I am simply after a little relief in my life, along with the reversal of a few bad habits we have fallen into – such as when Daphne says, 'If you just give me a candy cane then I'll stop yelling', and I seriously consider her offer. So, to cut down on hurt feelings and destroyed familial relationships, I've given everyone a new name and tweaked a few settings to protect the innocent. In fact, the only real names used in the book are those of Oona, Daphne and Mac. I have a feeling this book may disfigure a few of my friendships – I really hope I am wrong, as I love and admire and definitely empathize with all my friends with kids – but using real names would've done much more damage still. I rely on enormous generalizations in this book as a sort of shorthand, but I know that every country has its range of personalities.

Now, back to that giant landing pad for helicopter parenting, Park Slope, Brooklyn. Because, as it turns out, this part of the borough, and really most of Brooklyn, New York, provides an excellent environment for my undertaking. For starters, the French population is robust. The French and their well-behaved offspring are everywhere for me to behold – and study, interview and emulate. That's lucky because time is precious – and when our kids are young, every second counts even more. So why pack their days with play-dates and performances? When I was growing up, young children rarely took classes other than the Big Three: swimming, dance and piano. The swimming, by the way, was about waterproofing and not winning medals; dance was generally only for girls; and piano was related to discipline as much as anything else. Specialities like violin or football were offered to school-aged kids. Karate was truly exotic. Throw a rock in my neighbourhood today (though for the record I am not suggesting you do), and you'd likely hit an infant currently enrolled in yoga classes (baby yoga pants!), have it ricochet off him and tag a toddler who, thanks to rigorous instruction, can already communicate in sign language but maybe not yet talk, and finally wallop the head of a five-year-old psychoanalysis patient with a Mandarin language tutor. Poll the parents of these busy creatures about raising children in the twenty-first century, and the responses would likely refer to the confusing amount of choices, theories and products out there. Like parents of every generation, we love our children intensely – but we also have an unprecedented quantity of resources and information at our fingertips, and we wear ourselves out trying to give our children *everything*.

Wading through all the studies and expert theories, it is difficult to know what is best for our kids. One well-respected book says that the way to ensure a sense of independence in a child is to keep them *attached*, literally attached, to a parent (usually the mother) as much as their tiny hearts desire, until they feel completely ready and confident to face the world alone. Another leading contemporary theorist, meanwhile, insists that if a child isn't taught to play, soothe itself, and go to sleep independently, it will never have enough backbone to make it in this world. Both camps are convincing enough to confound any new parent.

As parents in today's society, we are accustomed to endless choices. With so many new ideas and opinions bouncing around us every day, it is no wonder that we race through parenting fads like nappies on a newborn. However, I've discovered that trying on a new parenting style when the first one fails can result in some rather calamitous fallout; I am surrounded by parents practically grovelling for approval from their children. It's painful to watch, and excruciating to be party to. It's not just happening in my home or in the smug, urban confines of my much written about Brooklyn neighbourhood – parenting throughout the English-speaking world is being dismantled. Evidence of an epidemic of confusion and misbehaviour can be seen in shopping malls, airports and petrol stations everywhere. Never mind our restaurants!

Ever since I had children, I've struggled with this

double-edged enlightenment. I found myself just wishing that someone, besides my mother, thank you very much, would tell me what really *worked*. My parents are religious Catholics, and most of their parenting decisions (like the one to have thirteen kids) were inspired by their faith. Which means that much of my mother's advice isn't really going to work on me, an acutely fallen disciple.

For all the reading and talking and web surfing I've done to try to figure out the best, most effective and yet loving and self-esteem-building approach to childrearing, you would think I really would have cracked the case by now. But instead, the results have been pointedly mixed.

One result of this is that, for the first four years of her existence, Daphne found her way to our bed *every* night. Another by-product: although my kids eat relatively well (that is, compared to many of their pals, who tend to consume only things that are white – mainly noodles, cheese and more noodles), dinnertime hardly resembles the organized, well-mannered family meals of my own youth; and, most of all, I am tired of negotiating over *everything*. I am very much not alone here. If I were given a penny every time I heard a parent apologize to a child, I would have enough to buy a new pair of toddler Ugg boots in no time at all.

Dissatisfied with both my children's, and my own, behavioural tendencies in the parent–child relationship, I began a little covert research. Basically, I'd fixate on any well-behaved child in a public setting and try to determine the grounds for its obedience. Generally, I try very hard to resist the urge to stereotype, but the more I dabbled in this line of covert research, the more often I discovered that the most governable little citizens I found were foreign. The more I thought about this and my exposure to my French friend Lucie and her children, the more I realized that, in an effort to find the right parenting style, most of my parent peers have buried a lot of valuable, tried and true techniques.

I needed to get French.

I've already introduced you to the three most important people in this story, but there are many others. *Il nous faut un village*, as Hillary Clinton might've said had she been born in Paris.

As mentioned earlier, there is no shortage of French families for me to investigate, as the French seem to be very fond of Brooklyn. In addition to the many French children who attend my daughters' school, there are abundant restaurants, boutiques and cafés teeming with willing subjects.

Then there is also France. *Que peut-on faire?* I just had to spend some time in the native land of the well-behaved. I just had to. Not sure I had to do *all* of that shopping in Paris, but again, what can one do? (In English that time.)

Luckily for me, the French are a proud people, and I have yet to encounter a Frenchie unwilling to discuss their inborn ways at length, with the exception of a trio of mothers at French/English storytime at a library on the Upper West Side of Manhattan, but I blame that on the bilingual American mom who poisoned them against me with her scepticism. Of course, I also had my inner circle of French confidantes, always available to guide me on my quest. However, although most French people are endowed with a healthy dose of pride, for the most part I find that they are also rather private, and so I've christened all the Frenchies in this book with new names as well.

As you will see, I turned to a veritable French army to help me navigate this brave new parenting world. But that's not to say that everything the French do I agree with and think we in the States and the UK should emulate. There is plenty we get right – I am a big believer in the can-do part of our cultural DNA. And I certainly don't suggest throwing the baby out with the bathwater – no matter how poorly behaved the baby might be.

For instance, although they discussed a spanking ban in French parliament a few years ago, *la fessée*, as it's called, is very much alive in France. Spanking is still legal in the States as well, but I saw more spanking in one week in France than I've seen in the last ten years in Brooklyn.

The paddle aside, it is not so surprising that I zeroed in on the French. My mother passed down to me a bit of Huguenot blood, and along with it boasting rights to a rebel affiliation with the French. Perhaps it is from her own grandmother, Rose Chabot (wait! That's her real name. New rule: the dead keep their given names in this book; the French love rules), that my mom acquired a respect of French customs. When I was a kid, both my parents would often point to the 'grace' and 'poise' of the French as something to behold – and imitate. When one of my brothers was born with a physical disability, out of all the holy sites in the world, my parents chose to take him to Lourdes in the French Pyrenees with the hope of landing a miracle. There was an attitude in the house I grew up in that the French knew how to do things right. I am sure that I've internalized this bias, and my feelings towards the French also developed into something a little stronger – a bit of a fetish, I'll admit. (But let's just call it a healthy case of Francophilia, shall we? Sounds much nicer and less suggestive of dungeon-dwelling spankers and thigh-high boots with too many buckles.) I first visited Paris when I was sixteen, and that's when the love truly took flight. It. Is. So. Beautiful. When I look around my home today, I count no less than eight replicas of the Eiffel Tower.

I knew I was going to marry my husband on our first Halloween together sixteen years ago, when he dressed up as Tintin, who, while technically the creation of a Belgian writer and illustrator, has been embraced most passionately by the French. (Oona, of course, recently discovered Tintin in our stacks and took to the stories like Captain Haddock takes to booze. I had to ask myself: How would a French parent respond when their six-year-old asks, 'What's an opium den?' Thanks a lot, Tintin.) At the baby shower for my first child, we received two copies of *The Red Balloon* in French, one in English, and then later came the Criterion Collection DVD of the film as well. My 'good' dinner service plates are the Pillivuyt Brasserie Collection, featuring the original menus – with prices in francs – of French restaurants and cafés from the 1920s.

My Francophilia spiked even higher when I began looking to the French for parenting wisdom. Early on in my quest, it took on strange forms and I began to see even my most quotidian experiences through Franco-tinted lenses. Last summer, for instance, the girls, Mac and I spent a week on the New Jersey shore. This was before I'd waded all that deeply into the French end of the parenting pool, so we acquiesced when the kids said they would rather swim in the overly chlorinated and packed hotel pool than in the wide open ocean, which beckoned only a couple of hundred feet away. But the French approach was very much on my mind.

We'd sit on the side, dangling our feet and ankles in the weirdly warm water while Daphne called, 'Look at me, Mommy! I'm a shark, Mommy!' and Oona hollered, 'Watch me go down the slide, Daddy!'

Over and over again. And then once more. Oh, OK, and then once more.

It was while sitting there one afternoon that I eaves-dropped on a handful of older kids – young teens – playing a pool game. From what I could gather, here's how the game worked: one kid held the wall at one side of the pool, with all the others grouped at the far end. The lone swim-mer – or catcher in the tide, if you will – gave the group a topic: favourite film, say, or favourite food. The group then decided among themselves on one collective answer and told the catcher to guess what it was. When the catcher guessed correctively – *Ace Ventura* – the group of swim-mers took off for the opposite wall, and the catcher tried to . . . catch as many of them as he could.

I watched the game progress with mild curiosity, and in between the implored Daphne/shark viewings, until one round sucked in my interest. The category was favourite food.

Catcher: 'Chicken!' No one in the group budged. Catcher: 'Chicken parm!' No budging. Catcher: 'Chicken parm with linguini!' The group practically emptied the pool of water, their paddling was so explosive.

Chicken parm with linguini? That's their favourite food? And the catcher knew that? Perhaps this is a regional anomaly – but somehow I don't think so. It is more likely that all across the States, small packs of teen swimmers are splashing about, incited by the mere mention of chicken parm with linguini.

Before I knew it, sitting there at this New Jersey motel pool, my mind wandered far beyond the Atlantic. Perhaps, at that exact moment, a similar game was going down in a hotel pool on the western coast of France. Only, instead of chicken parm with noodles, it went something like this: *Duck! Duck Margaret! Duck Margaret avec sauce orange!* I remember thinking that it might not be too late to shape kids who turn into young teens with sophisticated tastes and interesting ideas about food. Of course, the French don't say 'duck'. I had a lot of work ahead of me.

I never did find out what kind of swimming pool games French kids play, but I unearthed much, much more.

Incredibly, for an American mom used to fast-changing parenting trends, French childrearing techniques seem not to have changed all that much over the years. In some ways this can be scary – that whole spanking business – but in most others I have to say it is a relief. What new mom or dad, after all, has not been utterly baffled by the teeming shelves of the local bookshop's parenting section. Even the simplest seeming question – how the hell do I get my kid to sleep through the night? – morphs into a bloody battleground of conflicting information. No pressure, though: choose the wrong approach and you are only setting your kid up for a life of misery, abject failure, and – *mon Dieu!* – a non-Ivy League education.

The best part? We are expected to make these incredibly huge, life-altering decisions while experiencing terrorist suspect levels of sleep deprivation. It's a wonder any of us parents at all make it through alive – never mind the kids.

So, as you might imagine, I quite literally cried tears of immense, body-shaking joy when, five years into parenthood, I suddenly began to think there might be another way. A French way.

Was every idea suggested by my posse of French informants a resounding success? Of course not. Was I able to implement all the good advice I received? You're a parent – or know one – you tell me.

But this much is unequivocally true: after surprisingly little Frenchifying time, Daphne's McEnroe moments were diminishing (not much to be done about those Belushi tendencies – the kid is spirited!). There was also a perceptible decrease in Oona's supercilious eye-rolling. Now, as I write this, many months and months into the big experiment, the girls themselves are even exhibiting an unmistakable fondness for the French. We've talked about spending a future summer *en* Paris – and both girls light up thinking about *just how delicious* the pastries will be. Not long ago, Oona discovered the French–English dictionary on our bookshelf and started thumbing through it with great interest. Soon after, my husband and I heard her giggling over the palm-sized book in the next room. What, we asked her, could be so funny in a dictionary? She demurred for a moment, uncertain if she should share her finding. She feared we would think it was inappropriate for a seven-year-old. That's OK, we assured her, just tell us.

OK, she said, drawing a breath: 'C'est une garce.' Translation: He/she is a bitch.

Oona and Daphne cackled and did a little dance together, delighting in the tiny transgression. The French had done what not long ago seemed impossible: they'd brought Edith Wharton and Belushi together.

What other miracles were they capable of? I was determined to find out.

2

Un Début Français or French from the Start

My God. I love this place.

I often feel that way when I'm in Paris, but my heart practically exploded when a pregnant French friend announced that she was skipping the salad course at our lunch out in Montmartre. With a glass of red wine in hand because 'the iron is good for the baby', she explained, 'In France, we try to limit the raw, especially green leafy vegetables.' If I am ever pregnant again (the longest of long shots), I am so going to be French about it. I like vegetables as much as the next woman – maybe even more depending on who I am standing next to – but when I was pregnant I hated them with a zeal usually reserved for things like blisters or bad haircuts. I was nauseated all through both my pregnancies and really would have been happy eating nothing but instant mashed potatoes and oatmeal. However, I obsessively choked down as much kale, chard and romaine as I possibly could. For the baby! I would have dutifully done the same with goats' eyeballs if someone told me I had to – for the baby.

In retrospect, it is almost embarrassing that it took me so long to pay attention to the French. I should have known it the moment I began reading *The New Basics* by Dr Michel Cohen (a Frenchman, of course). After a steady diet of the utterly alarmist *What to Expect* books and the all too tender sentiments of the Sears family of paediatric writers ('attachment parenting', anyone?), I was ready for the direct, far more laissez-faire attitude of *le bon docteur*. Perhaps the name 'Gina Ford' will evoke this same reaction for Brits. I was eight months pregnant with my first child when a friend, a childless pal now that I think about it, randomly sent me the book, which presents Cohen's take on the early years of childrearing. I read it eagerly and then, when I'd finished, I did what any other American mother would do – I read about eight more books on the topic. Because that is how we do it – we approach pregnancy like a job, gobbling up everything we can on the subject so that we are experts on every theory. And, as with most jobs, a certain amount of drudgery accrues. I have discovered that, in addition to a mastery of these theories, this strategy to parenting also, unfortunately, results in utter confusion and frustration.

In the introduction, Cohen writes, 'I hope that reading this book will help you relax as a parent.' The book came out just one month before my first child was born, but it took me nearly seven years to really pay attention. Relax! Such a simple idea, and yet one I'd completely overlooked whenever my baby developed even a low-grade fever or a hint of diarrhoea or, heaven forbid, dropped her soother out of reach of a sterilizer.

Now, as I am going back through all of the literature I had consumed in the early years, trying to figure out how my generation of parents arrived in our current state of tumult with our kids, I see some of what I missed. The directive gleaned in entry after entry from the good French doctor suggests that we all just chill out a little. For instance, here is what he has to say to parents that worry about bowed legs: 'I don't know of any babies with straight legs. They all have slight bowing, and some have a little more than others. But their legs always straighten with age, although some adults keep a slight residual bowing, which is of no concern, especially if you're a cowboy.' This is the tone of his book, and I love it. And Cohen's book, written for Americans, is like an inflamed polemic compared to the baby manuals most French parents-to-be consult.

I well remember when my sister called me in tears towards the end of her second pregnancy. She was worried sick about her two-year-old, who would be deprived of so much of her time and devotion when the new baby arrived. I spewed out everything I had read about helping an older sibling adjust to a new baby, like having special items on hand so big brother doesn't feel left out, or planning alone time after the baby is born, and instructing visitors bringing gifts to the newborn to pick up something for the older kid as well. My sister was so hysterical about the pain she might cause her beloved firstborn that she had me in tears too. Then I read what Cohen had to say on the matter: he advises not to do any of the things I had told my sister to do, not to excuse any bad behaviour on the part of the older child when baby enters the picture, and certainly not to feel sorry for anyone involved. Siblings are great. The firstborn *should* – and will – be pleased to have a brother or sister. He's so right . . . and so French.

For me, the moment I learned I was pregnant was, not at all coincidentally, the moment I added a new manic energy to my personality. This was no trifling matter: ask anyone who's seen me do my best breakdance move, 'the worm', on a disco floor. But now, I had so many new things to worry me. Well-intended citizens from all corners of my life cautioned me about everything from tap water to eggs to nail varnish to emotional stressors. War films might be too much to handle. I was afraid to open my mouth for a bite, or even a breath, without first consulting an expert. One friend had me fearful that the subway's screeches at my Manhattan transfer would detrimentally affect my poor little zygote's developing eardrums. I am not, by nature, a neurotic person, but the onslaught of angst was impossible to deflect. 'Woman,' this Chorus of Agita sang in a dreadful loop, 'the world is no place for little people.' (I prefer the more reasonable line by Nicolas Cage's character H. I. McDunnough in the film *Raising Arizona*: 'Sometimes it is a hard world for small things.' OK, yes, that character is not exactly a paragon of parenting – he did, after all, end up in a high-speed car chase after stealing some nappies – but there is a certain pragmatism I admire in that line. The world is not always hard on small things – just sometimes.)

While, for the most part, I wouldn't say that the French are careless with their little *in utero* visitors, they are certainly a lot less anxious than what I've seen from expectant moms on this side of the pond, here in the States. Over and over, when I spoke with pregnant French women, I noted a distinct lack of that '*ohmygod ohmygod ohmygod, breathe!*' feeling that is so familiar in my social circle.

OK, not all French women breeze through pregnancy – one woman from Brittany confessed to me, 'I do think I should probably eat less of the steak tartare.'

Less steak tartare? When I last checked, steak tartare was raw meat. Raw meat, I should point out, that once had me hurling all over Montparnasse years before the kids were born. As a preggers person, meanwhile, I was instructed, by way of the *What to Expect* 'Best Odds' diet, not to eat rice. Rice. As the diet was supposed to give me the best odds of having a healthy baby, when I couldn't comply I was reduced to tears. Yet white rice represented one of three or four things that wouldn't make me spew. What a cretin I felt like for indulging . . . in rice.

From what my foreign confidantes revealed, the average French obstetrician makes the earlier mentioned Dr Cohen seem like an alarmist. While it is true that these days even most pregnancy manuals *en Française* warn against any with-child alcohol or cigarette consumption, advice being offered in the more comfy confines of the doctor's office is less strict. This is what a few pregnant French women told me when I asked after their imbibing habits:

> 'My doctor asked me to limit to one glass of wine with a meal, only two cups of coffee every day, and only three cigarettes each day, if I have to – although he doesn't want me to smoke. So I don't – except once in a while.'

> 'My French doctor said I could eat whatever I wanted but only one glass of wine each day.'

> 'My obstetrician is very strict about drinking and not eating. Only wine with food.'

Over and over, French women told me about these 'restrictions'. It could be a fluke, but I've not found one American with a doctor who sanctioned a daily alcoholic drink. When my obstetrician said I could have three drinks, I made her repeat herself. On the second go-around, I realized that she meant I could have three drinks throughout *my entire* pregnancy. She relented, 'Have a glass of champagne on your anniversary, or maybe a glass of wine on your birthday, something during the holidays. That will be OK.' Gee, thanks.

It sounds as if doctors in the UK, while not quite as strict as their American colleagues, do follow certain guidelines. While advising against drinking at all, the NHS allows its harried mothers-to-be 'one to two units of alcohol once or twice a week'.

On paper, the French are not so different from us, and in 2007 it was even mandated that all alcoholic beverages sold in France come with a label stating that the consumption thereof could be harmful to the health of the unborn child. In practice, though, things are still a bit different. Maybe it's because, as many people have pointed out, those French warning labels are teeny tiny.

In any event, the occasional glass of wine would seriously change my attitude towards pregnancy. It sure would've helped to know that one was at the end of another long day that started with extreme morning sickness, as well as take the sting off the pregnancy-induced carpal tunnel that had me in wrist braces with both kids. I may even have kicked fewer puppies had a daily, or even weekly, glass of vino been on the table. (Note to my kids: I've never actually kicked a puppy.)

I am no doctor or even scientifically minded, so I am not going to pick sides here. I do know first-hand that the Irish are a little closer to the French attitude (shocker, I know). When I was seven or eight months pregnant, some pals visited me from Dublin. As it happens, my visiting Irish friends called their New York Irish friends, and I found myself in a bar brimming with Irish. At least six times, I heard some version of this: '*Ah Catrin! Nice ter meet yer. Let me buy yer a draink.*' Since I was sitting down, I'd give them the benefit of the doubt and decline the kind offer while pointing to my extended abs. The inevitable response: '*Ah, den let me git yer a beer.*' Then again, I am not sure if anyone should let an Irish attitude towards the drink inform their decisions while pregnant. Still, the fact remains, if you are pregnant in the States (even if you Skype with a French OBGYN), one of the best reasons to avoid drinking is that someone might see you with a baby on board and a drink in hand and physically assault you.

I recently heard of an American doctor who, upon seeing one of her pregnant patients indulging in a small glass of wine, proclaimed: 'Well, I hope you're happy. You just gave your baby foetal alcohol syndrome. You now have to live with that for the rest of your life.'

This American doc might need a shot of Pinot herself. She's probably done more damage to the psyche of her patient than any harm this pregnant woman did to her child with the wine. I am not saying that expectant women should get tanked up to the point that they wake up in some stranger's bed off the coast of Naples (although that does sound sort of sweet) but, rather, just reconsider the bone-dry approach. Or, even better, just try to avoid turning into a complete basket case about everything.

I have even come across the argument that a little womb service red wine (it's always red) advantageously affects the brain development of a baby. I don't know if I buy that, but I like to read about it none the less.

In speaking with French mothers about the medical advice they received while pregnant, as well as the books they consulted, I found that a common difference between the French approach and the American temperament is the distribution of focus. Here, we are pretty zeroed in on the foetus. It is understandable to want to grow a healthy baby, but the whole industry is so wrought with anxiety here that it can be a bit staggering. Early in my first pregnancy, my husband and I went straight into defence mode. Test the tap water! Test the paint! Remove all plastic serving-ware from the house! Interview nannies! Interview vitamins! Avoid shellfish! Avoid shelves! And on and on.

It is not that the French don't make adjustments, but they also don't seem as completely consumed by the miracle within. Probably the most famous French author on the subject of maternity is Madame Laurence Pernoud, whose two books *J'attends un enfant* (*I Am Expecting a Child*) and *J'élève mon enfant* (*I Bring Up My Child*) have sold tens of millions of copies, and that is not counting any of the translated versions. The wife of Georges Pernoud, an editor with *Paris-Match*, Madame Pernoud first decided to write an advice book about pregnancy and motherhood when she found herself expecting for the first time at the age of thirty-five, and could not find a book that answered her questions. It seems she was not alone, and French women have turned to her ever since *J'attends un enfant* was first published in 1956. In fact, neither of Pernoud's two most prominent books has ever gone out of print. There have been many editions, additions and revisions to the books over the years, but the basis of her advice has held strong, including her instruction in areas such as staying beautiful, eating fresh butter, and keeping the boobs perky. Well, all right: priorities!

Pernoud's publishers are perpetually releasing new versions of her books, so you can imagine that the bookstores in France are saturated with her wisdom. The story is not the same in the United States, where copies of her books are almost impossible to find. I did, however get my hands on the 2002 edition of *J'élève mon enfant*, in which she still encourages expectant mothers to remain the 'coquette' and insists that regular beauty rituals are essential to good morale.

And what was that advice about keeping boobs perky? Laurence Pernoud reminds her audience how important it is to keep them *très fermes*. After weaning my own kids, I developed the notion that the federal government should offer any woman who has breast-fed two or more children the automatic right to a boob lift. Even fiscal conservatives must see how this would help keep married couples together, thus providing a long-term, trickling-down financial benefit to the country. If Pernoud were president, we might even have a chance. (Sadly, she was not born in the USA and thus could never hold the high office. Also, she died in 2009. RIP.) My fantasy bill will probably never reach Capitol Hill. Now, I just wish I could go back in time and heed Pernoud's advice. It is obvious stuff, but when I was pregnant I was so focused on what was going on inside my body, it never occurred to me to worry about what might happen to my exterior. In her chapter 'Taking Care of Your Breasts', Pernoud explains how the pectoral muscles, when properly exercised, can help to keep your bosom aloft, or at least in check. I well remember advice, seemingly coming from every direction, to keep up with the dreaded kegels. (According to urbandictionary.com: 'the name of a pelvic floor muscle and exercise, named after Dr Kegel who discovered the exercise. These muscles are attached to the pelvic bone and act like a hammock, holding in your pelvic organs. A common function of these muscles is stopping and starting the flow of urine. In men, the benefits of kegel exercises include increased ejaculatory control. In women, a strong kegel muscle can aid in efficient childbirth and gives the vagina a better grip.') Meanwhile, no one suggested I work out the upper-deck. As it was, since I had C-sections with both my deliveries, all that kegel advice was for naught. In addition to offering actual breast perkiness exercises, and sounding very motherly indeed, Pernoud reminds her readers to simply 'stand up straight, with your shoulders slightly back . . . emphasizing your breasts'. This will help keep the ta tas looking lively, and it will also reduce back pain.

My husband and I, and yes, the ta tas, too, thank you, Madame Pernoud.

I find Pernoud's shared focus between mother and baby rather refreshing, and it probably has a lot to do with why new French mothers tend to look less stressed and befogged than the ones I see haunting my neighbourhood. If I have learned nothing else in my

Frenchification research, it is that the French are experts at self-preservation, even as their precious bundles grow and develop the ability to demand more from their moms.

But I am getting ahead of myself, because Pernoud does not stop with perky breasts. She devotes impressive space in her book to 'staying pretty'. The American-authored pregnancy books I read practically screamed at me for having the temerity to wear nail varnish, which is why I look completely distressed and undone (in every sense of the word) in all but two of my pregnancy photos. Meanwhile, pregnant French women get make-up lessons and coaching on how to dress.

Pregnant or not, I'm not sure I'd want to take the fashion advice of anyone born before the invention of short-wave radio, but that's not really the point here. The fact that Pernoud includes these issues is a welcome change from all the worry and pressure (and lack of style advice) that comes along with being preggers in the States.

I've discovered that being pregnant in France has other advantages: one of my favourite dinner party facts is that, post childbirth, French women are entitled to ten free sessions of 'pelvic floor rehabilitation' as well as follow-up, on the house, abdominal therapy – to get the tummy back in couture shape.

Yes, they take their pregnant citizens very seriously

in France. To wit: an American friend of mine, Ramona, had the good fortune of moving to France just before she got knocked up. When she began showing, Ramona found herself often scolded by other French women for not taking advantage of the liberties that come along with pregnancy. That is, they thought she should be more comfortable 'playing the pregnant card'. The first time she really got reamed was queuing up for the fitting rooms at a Parisian department store. An older woman demanded of her: 'Why are you waiting in the queue? You are pregnant! You go to the front! It is your right! It is the law!' It was then that Ramona realized the French really wanted her to jump the queue, and that by waiting like a ordinary citizen she was somehow messing up the rules for everyone else. After that, Ramona was more than happy to comply. She wrote to me enthusiastically: 'THIS ROCKS. I have four months left of this card, and goddammit, I am using every last one. Move over, *biatches*, I got twelve items on a seven item limit and I got a giant dressing room and I will happily push past your size 0 ass BECAUSE I CAN.'

Meanwhile, as a massively pregnant woman I found myself crying on a crowded New York City subway because no one offered me a seat. I remember denouncing all of humanity one day on my commute home from the office when the only thing that I wanted in the world was to sit down and survive (i.e. not vomit). I was clearly very pregnant and I must have looked green around the gills, yet no one even looked me in the eyes to notice that the tears were welling up, not to mention offered me a seat. I thought maybe this was a behavioural problem unique to the Big Apple, but I've had friends from Chapel Hill in North Carolina to Notting Hill in London lament the fact that they received no special treatment with pounds and pounds of foetus and fluid attached to their mid-sections.

For many Americans, the big pregnancy perk is a baby shower. Finally, you get some props! And presents! And virgin punch. Oy. Yet, this is something that the French do not enjoy. Take it from my friend Jessie. She was born in France, spent her formative years in California, and then moved back to France as an adult. When Jessie was pregnant with her first child, she inquired among her French friends about a baby shower – and was instead given 'the evil eye'. She discovered that the French regard it as very bad taste and highly tacky to expect gifts for a baby that isn't even born. Maybe this lack of baby showers accounts for the fact that the list of suggested items for a new baby in France is considerably shorter, and ultimately less exasperating, than what's customary in the States. It seems the French list of items to stockpile for a new baby includes less entries than my mid-week grocery list.

The first time I looked at a list of suggested items to register for while pregnant, I felt as if I was alone on the receiving end of an out-and-out attack. I remember having to leave Babies R Us before I had a panic attack.

To go with my new baby, I would apparently need no

less than an additional apartment in which to house its gear. I told myself I would not succumb to the pressure, but somehow I ended up with three pushchairs (one high-quality, one fold-up job for travel, and a jogger, of course), a bassinette, Moses basket, pack-n-play, co-sleeper, crib, free-standing swing, ExerSaucer, play mat, doorway swing, both regular audio and closed-circuit baby monitors (I live in a stairless apartment!), a Baby Bjorn, a sling, a Mayan Wrap (which should have come with a distinguished PhD candidate to help decipher the instructions), at least seventeen baby blankets and, sadly, shamefully, a wipe warmer. A wipe warmer, for those lucky enough not to know, is just what it sounds like: a brick-sized device whose sole purpose is to heat baby wipes to a temperature that will not upset, alarm or disturb your infant's back section in even the slightest way. This creation may be the best proof yet that untethered innovation is not always the answer.

Maybe it is from all of the processed foods in this country or maybe it is hormones, but something odd happens to the American brain when we start to breed, and our weakness for stuff, stuff and more stuff gets further inflated. Take my youngest brother, one of the thriftiest people I know. Ben and his wife *shared* a mobile phone for almost five years! They weren't short on funds, mind you, it's just that my brother does not like waste – be it water, money or the latest in telecommunications (I think he still owns only two pairs of shoes, and one pair is flip-flops). That is, he was miserly with any and everything – until his wife was with child. I screamed out loud at my computer monitor when I first read that my tightfisted little *frère* had registered for a $600 pram. Even the strongest among us go soft in the head prepartum. And post-partum too, of course (much more on that later).

With Pernoud's pruned list in mind, now take a look at what is typically recommended for the American mother to stockpile. If you have already lived through this particular brand of torture, I apologize for the recurrence of any post-traumatic stress. Alright, if you aren't sitting already, you may want to. Grab a sandwich. Fluff up a pillow under yourself. Get comfy. Here goes:

Breast pump

Breast milk storage bags

Three receiving blankets of ample size

Car seat

Extra car seat bases if you have more than one car

Stroller that can push around car seat

Newborn sleep station: Moses basket or co-sleeper

Pack and Play with the bassinette insert

Pack and Play sheets – differently sized than crib sheets

Sling

Front carrier

Swing

Bouncy seat

Infant bathtub

Nappy bag

Nursing pillow

Boppy

Baby monitor

Crib

Crib mattress sold separately

Crib sheets – three sets

Crib bumper

Mobile for crib

Mobile for above the changing table

Extra changing pad

Changing pad covers

Two fluffy bath towels

Sun shades for car windows

Bottle drying rack

Receptacle for bottle pieces

Glider/rocker

Changing table and dresser

Newborn clothing:

  2–4 infant gowns

  4–8 bodysuits or onesies

  4–8 undershirts or vests

  4–8 one-piece pyjamas

  2 blanket sleepers

  1–3 sweaters or jackets

  1–3 rompers or other dress-up outfits

  4–7 pairs of socks or booties

  4–6 hats

  Mittens bunting bag or fleece suit

Toys

Nail clippers

Digital thermometer

Washcloths

Burp cloths

Medicines: Baby Tylenol, Baby Orajel, Baby Mylicon, Gripe
 Water

Baby shampoo and body wash

Nappy rash ointment

Purell

Soothers with clips/leashes

Large maxi pads

Disposable breast pads

Nipple cream

Newborn nappies – just one pack in case your baby is huge
 and outgrows 'em right away!

Size one nappies

Nappy bin

Nappy bin liners

Nappy service

Nappy wipes with refills

Nappy wipes warmer (Argh!)

Formula

Formula dispenser

Bottle brush

Bottles – two sizes (4 oz and 8 oz)

High chair or booster/feeding chair

Booster seat for car

Sturdy pushchair for when baby can sit up

Feeding bowls, spoons

Bibs

Activity table

ExerSaucer
Hallway jumper

I swear to you that this isn't just a list of all of the baby paraphernalia I could think of. I did not want to rely solely on (the faulty) memories of my own pregnancies, so I checked in with a number of folk around the States in the middle of the pre-baby 'gathering' period. This is a distillation of what's happening on today's baby registry circuit. I collapsed toys and left out a few of the more ridiculous entries – homeopathic teething tablets, cleaning service, night nurse – because I do have some pride in my people, but you get the idea. We are obsessed! I am not saying less is more – because it's not; it is less. I am saying that less could very well be a good thing.

So, beware Britannia. I fear that these materialistic nesting tendencies have bled across the Atlantic. It's a slippery slope.

Unless you have a boatload of time on your hands, you might want to avoid an internet search of the words 'baby registry'. It will yield not only countless sites devoted to instructing hapless new moms and dads on exactly what they should list, but also a slew of posts from unnerved registrants, completely stressed out by the process as they are not sure of the best bottle, crib sheet fabric, organic formula, or highly stimulating mobile to sign up for. It is utterly overwhelming, and largely unnecessary. As if carrying the baby around in utero is not enough, we pile it on with the added burden of worry that we aren't going to get the (many, many, oh so many) supplies right. It is a nice idea to shower new parents with necessities for an expanding family, but in the process we have created a climate of apprehension, bordering on panic.

Valerie, a mom friend from Brittany, pointed out to me how much expectant women count on the government to make their baby-carrying time not just bearable, but even almost pleasurable (again, some American moms may like being preggers – not me). She told me:

> [it is] really important to consider how people are cared for in general by the government here. The state gives all pregnant women a subsidy of 150€ a month starting at the 4th month of pregnancy if she visits her doctor (absolutely free through childbirth, including a hospital stay for up to a week) once a month during the pregnancy. This subsidy continues until the child turns eighteen if the mother has more than one child. This is true for all women no matter their income. Women also have sixteen full weeks of paid maternity leave by law for the first child and more for successive children. I have two children, fourteen and seventeen, and I still receive monthly 'family benefits'. So, in the end, perhaps baby showers would be superfluous.

Touché.

Childcare Cash Benefits in France

In 2008, when Brad Pitt and Angelina Jolie relocated to the breathtaking Chateau Miraval in the south of France, they became eligible for these kinds of benefits, available to any family no matter how much they are worth. The website bittenandbound.com broke it down:

> Although it is unlikely Brad and Angelina will cash in, they are technically eligible for a 'nanny payment' of $975.84 a month to help with childcare, and an 'orphan allowance' of $508.97 for each of their three adopted children. The $2,592.81 total would be payable by cheque each month.

As if having Brad Pitt and a chateau wasn't enough – AJ gets a *nanny payment*! Consider me green.

Amid this atmosphere of angst, it is also no wonder that we Americans tend to approach the baby's arrival with overblown trepidation.

Here I'll admit that I was utterly terrified. The frequent peeing in my pants was not only due to the extra weight on my bladder, but to everything I imagined might go wrong. What if we forgot to bring our birth plan? What if they give me drugs? What if they don't give me drugs? Why didn't I go for the water birth? But if I did, what if the baby drowned? The worries never ended. And then, there was the constant mental torment about what would happen after the baby was born. This is what I, and scores of expectant mothers, do with our energy.

This mass of anxiety, which is so common, has led many an American mother-to-be to draft up 'instructions' on how they would like their families and friends to behave in the early days after a baby's birth. I came across one blog post that was so overwrought and jumpy – including everything from the use of antibacterial to what kind of comments directed at baby and mother are acceptable – that my own knuckles were white after reading it. This poor first-time mom was already so severely chafed, weeks before her child was due – and I don't mean the kind of thing that any nipple cream can soothe (although I am betting she has a few tubes – it's a popular registry item). By worrying about everything from germs to breast exposure to the fact that her baby might be funny looking, she had done, in her emotionally fragile state, a bang-up job of taking the fun out of things. Let me lean on my pal Pernoud one more time here, because, in *J'attends un enfant*, she advises her minions of French moms not to talk about giving birth with any friends who have gone through it, and to save such conversations for the doctor. Although I am not in total agreement here, we could tone it down a little. Sometimes I worry that my mom friends and I do little more than scare one another. For instance, at one point I was utterly petrified that Oona was going to have inferior peripheral vision because she would not tolerate 'tummy time' as an infant. I had latched on to something a friend told me she'd read, and then successfully turned myself into a nervous wreck. It wasn't until I thought to consult Dr Cohen that I calmed down. Incidentally, Dr Cohen points out that it is totally normal for babies to reject being placed on their bellies as, to ward off sudden infant death syndrome, they are always on their backs. He very calmly advises: 'Since there is no need to strengthen any specific muscle group, I advise you not to act as Lucy's [any female baby in Cohen speak] personal trainer. Skip the tummy time, and tickle her tummy so she'll exercise her giggling muscles instead.' Aah – so much better than being terrified to the point of insomnia.

Speaking of horror films, consider the $250 million industry born from the cord blood controversy. Do not avert your eyes! The instant I went public with my pregnancy, I began receiving all kinds of brochures and emails about saving my newborn's cord blood. Every time I turned around I was bombarded with information, and pressure, from the cord blood banking companies. The marketing campaigns are not subtle, suggesting, as they do, that if parents do not choose to retrieve their newborn's cord blood and store it at this company's facilities for years to come, they *just might* be dooming one of their children who *just might* develop a crappy disease in the future that *just might* be treatable with the stockpiled cord blood. There is so much fear and guilt involved with these advertisements it's impossible to escape them without completely freaking out. I should know – I didn't. I was not in a financial position to sign up for the service, but I felt like a terrible mother crossed with an ogre (a mogre?) at the thought of not freezing my innocent little baby's umbilical blood. Additionally, every time I saw one of those cord blood flyers I was newly petrified by the thought of all those awful diseases that might attack my child. Leukaemia, polio, gout, haemorrhoids, club foot, Chicago Cubs fandom – you name it, and I was in fear. Yet, in the end, we didn't go for it. When my pregnant friends came to me in hysteria over their own cord blood banking decisions, I didn't really know what to tell them. That is, until I discovered that private cord blood banking is illegal in France for anyone not at risk and pregnant French women are never terrorized over the matter.

For one thing, the French see the cord blood as a national resource, and so parents are encouraged to donate their baby's cord blood to a public bank at birth (we have them in the States, too, by the way). But it's not really clear how effective the stored blood and cells can be for treating the child later in life. In fact, in many instances of disease, a child's own cells are the last ones that should be used for treatment.

Had I a keener eye on the French when I was pregnant, I would have been much more serene about the whole thing. Those Frenchies are all about keeping it simple. I wish I could go back in time with more of the French approach in mind. I imagine enjoying Gruyère more (Pernoud especially recommends this delightful cheese for pregnant women) and less of a need for a push-up bra.

A French Frame of Mind

I haven't done much acting in my life, except for one appearance as Hodel in *Fiddler on the Roof* as a high school freshman, but I imagine that if I ever ventured to crack the boards, I would totally go method (like Shelley Winters) – a conclusion I reached in my attempts to act French.

To get into the mood, I started swapping in some choice French terms of endearment when I was otherwise about to drop a 'darling' or 'sweetie'. Maybe it was my imagination, but I swear I was more successful saying things like: 'This is the only dinner you are going to get, *mon petit chou*, so do not leave the table until you are truly finished.'

Here's a little chart to get you started. Feel it!

French term	Translation	Use it for . . .
Mon Petit Chou	My Little Cabbage	Sweetheart
Ma Puce	My Flea	Boo Boo
Ma Crotte	My Dropping	Sweet Pea
Ma Caille	My Quai	Little Man
Mon Lapin	My Rabbit	Bunny
Ma Cherie	My Dear	Darling

NO TRANSLATION: Buddy

Obvious honourable mentions:

Mon Ange
Mon Bébé
Mon Amour

3

Vous Êtes le Chef or On Becoming the Chief

I can guess what you're wondering: if the French are so relaxed, why are their children so obedient?

While French children in Brooklyn are well behaved, the French kids in their native land politely run circles around them. On my most recent trip to Paris, I was, once again, shocked to find that I had to specifically look for them (to study them!), because most of these little citizens are truly seen and not heard. I travelled amazed on a silent metro car after realizing that there were many children on board. They were just sitting there, not fidgeting or demanding toys and snacks. Just sitting. The same goes for the museums – the few times I encountered a tantrum, it was invariably coming from a pint-sized British or American tourist, not a French child. I thought for sure I'd get some action in the supermarkets – I mean, what kind of kid can resist the temptation of shelves of treats? Apparently, French kids. And their decorum in restaurants? It's almost enough to make you stab their happily unbothered parents in the throat with a steak knife. Almost.

So how do they do it? How do French parents manage to keep their children so well behaved?

The answer is a bit complicated, but parental attitudes on child psychology play a large role. For instance, the fact that multiple French parents have told me that the 'Terrible Twos' do not exist in their country makes me wonder if it is such an enormous deal here because we British and American parents consider this stage in development a *fait accompli*.

Yes, you read that right – NO SUCH THING AS THE TERRIBLE TWOS! When I first heard this, I thought my French informant was just, well, uninformed. But then I heard it over and over. I even had to explain the concept itself to a few of my French contacts. One, my friend Paul, was mystified when I translated the meaning: 'Really? You have this with your children. I have never heard of this condition.' It should be noted that Paul said this while he was baking a fresh peach tatin *with my children*.

Before I even gave birth, I was well versed on this phase because practically every book I read warned of its inevitability, with some going so far as to explain this 'developmental stage' in scientific terms. Even my own father-in-law (a psychiatrist admittedly obsessed with brain function) had me deeply perturbed when he described the 'chemical brainwash' that would take place when my sweet unborn baby entered her second year of life and her brain experienced a growth spurt leading to hormonal chaos as nerve connections fired inside her forming brain. I can't say that I ever really understood what anyone was talking about; the only thing that really sunk in was that I should be afraid, very afraid.

So, on cue, when Daphne and Oona both developed into two-year-old lunatics, I chalked it up to those unavoidable 'Terrible Twos'. How could I fight with nature? We just had to endure – at least that's what I believed. In hindsight, this left the Turbid Threes and Frightful Fours totally unexplained.

But back to the 'complicated' answer. Then there is the reality that the French still rely heavily on extended family in the raising of their kids. In fact, throughout my investigation, I've found that new French parents are much more likely to turn to their own parents and grandparents for childcare advice rather than to books or websites, as we do here, and this has everything to do with the fact that their extended families often live nearby and play a significant role in bringing up *les enfants*. Even *way* out in the countryside, the French are less nomadic than we itinerant Americans. A friend of a friend, Simon, lives in the Vosges mountain range on the eastern tip of France. That is to say, boon-f*** nowhere. Although he is an Englishman, he has been living in France for decades and has a daughter with a French woman. Simon noted that the people in his village don't tend to move very far from their families. 'I've had the same postman for eight years,' he marvels. He also mentioned that he can't remember the last time he saw a child throw a tantrum 'excluding my trips home to England, that is'. This will never cease to amaze me.

America is the land of independence and entrepreneurs – we stray from the coop in significant ways, be it for jobs, love or dreams. When we land, we are often completely removed from where we started (just look at me, a California girl who has clocked nearly fifteen years in New York City). One of the reasons mothers' groups and mommy blogs are so popular in the States is that we use them to fill the void of familial support. These web havens haven't captured the imaginations of French parents in the same way. The results of these different approaches are fascinating to behold. I remember urging my sister (who lives 4,500 kilometres away) to cut the cord with the group she began attending after the birth of her first son because it seemed as though the aftermath of every meeting involved her calling me with a new set of concerns about her baby. Rather than bringing support, this particular gathering became a breeding ground for worry. I know that not all such groups have this effect, but it's certainly more prevalent in the States than in France. My own husband tried to elicit a pledge from me to give up the blogs because he noted a similar pattern. I think it was when, after about two hours online, I'd awoken him in a panic, utterly convinced that one of our kids had colon cancer. It turned out to be a severe case of threadworms, by the way. When the French need a solution to a particular problem, they tend to consult one source, not fifteen different friends or chat-room chums. If nothing else, this has the effect of cutting down on anxiety – something that I'd discovered does wonders for just about every aspect of parenting but, unfortunately, something that we

Americans are far from mastering. Take heed, Britain, lest you lose your stiff upper lip and become as tormented as we are here.

When I tried going to a typical French source for solutions to specific behavioural transgressions, however, there was often something lost in translation:

Me: 'So what do you do when your child is having a fit in the grocery store?'

Veronique (French mom): 'What do you mean? Is my child hurt? Why is he having a fit?'

Me: 'I don't know. Any reason. You wouldn't get him the cereal he wanted, or he wants to push the shopping trolley or something.'

Veronique: 'Hmm. I don't think I understand. Did he hurt himself with the trolley and he is crying?'

Me: 'No, he's just crying because he didn't get his way.'

Veronique: 'In the grocery store? Non. He would not do that. The French do not really like that.'

The French don't like that? I don't like that!

Unfortunately, I was not always able to find a French-inspired solution to the attitudinal shortcomings of my kids because many of their behaviours just don't exist in the same way in France. The real trick – listen carefully all of you who have yet to spawn or have very small children – is to create the proper relationship with your children from the very beginning. Remember: YOU ARE

54

THE CHIEF. When I consider my own parenting trajectory, the main reason I wasn't able to discipline my kids effectively is that I did not want to inhibit their wonderful, budding personalities. I didn't want to tread on their individualism. This strikes me as a very American approach, and there is much merit to it, but perhaps not to the extremes that we have taken it. In France, everyone in the family has a job. The parents' role is to be the Chief and the children have the job of obeying their leader. French children are raised with this in mind, so there is much less debate and resistance. Just as in the previous chapter, when my pregnant friend was chastised for not taking her rightful place at the front of the line – 'It's the law!' – and fouling up the rules, French kids know that their business involves obeying adults. Ever since this was explained to me, I have been dropping it on my own daughters. It is kind of fun to say things like 'You will get in the car now and put on your seatbelt because I am the Chief and I said so.'

The crazy thing? It works. Initially, I was afraid that they would become resentful of my new assertions of power and tightened discipline, but that is not the case. They were so used to debating and arguing about everything – because I had raised them to think that their opinion on *everything* was important – that now they almost seemed relieved to have a real Chief take charge.

I like being the Chief, but to do it effectively I have had to become more strict, which is the hardest part for me. I have never been much good at saying 'no' to my kids and I have always gravitated to those in the parenting world who talk and write about 'the power of yes' and how important it is to respect children and their feelings. With two daughters, I've long held visions of the three of us as a happy little clique when they grow up, laughing in a café and swapping stories. Like a scene from a sloppy film. Cheesy I know, but hey, it sounds nice. I just really want my kids to like me. Now, French moms are pretty firm, yet from what I have seen they more often appear to have wonderful relationships with their adult daughters. Possibly this is because they have maintained some dignity in the eyes of their kids by not always seeming desperate for acceptance. One French mom broke it down for me in simple terms: 'Your job is not to be their friend. That does not work with children. You need to be their mom and teach them well. I would love to spend my day holding my child, but I know that is not good for him.' I have spent entire days holding my Daphne, congratulating myself that, at the very least, I was reducing the risk of her becoming a serial killer. Of course, I had read the *Attachment Parenting Book* by Dr William Sears, so avoiding raising murderesses was the very least I was going for – I was promised kids who would be more secure and smarter than those whose heartless parents had not elected to *wear* them. They would be easy to discipline, respectful, and a whole bunch of other wonderful qualities. Perhaps there's another reason for it, but the endless attention and energy that I bestowed upon my girls as babies and toddlers ultimately produced clingy and demanding little kids (as well as one strung-out mom). Practically every French mother that I have

encountered insists that enforcing discipline and cultivating self-restraint in children is the truest expression
of love.

Most of the French parents I spoke with divulged that
they read only a few, if any, books on parenting. However,
the author that many of them turned to is a doctor and
psychoanalyst named Françoise Dolto. Dolto, a bit of a
brainiac who worked with Jacques Lacan, preached the
importance of children having separate lives from those
of their parents. Amen, sister! Recently, my husband's
cousin arrived from out of town, and the only thing I
wanted was a little separation from my kids so that I
could catch up with the in-laws. But alas, darling Daphne
was in a full-on French relapse, and it wasn't until after I
brought her to bed that any of the adults could mean-
ingfully converse. Sadly, I was relegated to the bedtime
ritual, so I missed the heart of the homecoming. Too
many American kids are brought up thinking that their
every little utterance is precious and worthy of an audience – mine included, no doubt. As one French father
explained to me, 'Where I am from, we refer to the child
whose parents hang there on everything it says and does
as *l'enfant roi*. I think it is like your spoiled brat, maybe,
but not so bad. It is not the child's fault that the parents
treat it like a king.' I wanted to give my daughters confidence and a healthy sense of self-worth by validating
their achievements, but now they think that running
around the dining room table with three stuffed animals
in their shirts is fascinating to everyone. I had ended up
with a couple of show-offs who didn't know how to sit

and participate in a discussion without being the centre of it. I love them dearly, but there is truly nothing amazing about putting a couple of stuffies down one's front, and I want my kids to know it. Perhaps in the future, if this developed into a more compelling performance piece (with, like, the Coen brothers directing and a cameo from Jeff Bridges), then we'd have something. However, from the beginning, my daughters have known only the approval and attention of grown-ups, and it is hard for everyone involved to just turn off the tap. We are certainly working on it and making strides – leaps really with Oona.

Sadly, I can't say the same for all of my friends. I shudder at the memory of a summertime soirée we attended one year at the house of a dear friend, Bonnie, on the Upper West Side of Manhattan. Bella, Bonnie's nearly eight-year-old daughter, had a vision for a parlour game, so before the party, mother and daughter sent emails to the four families attending, asking us all to bring a special object and to be prepared to tell a story about it. Already, this seemed rather unFrench to me but, for starters, we don't live in France, so my husband and I complied. The party was lovely, made even lovelier by Bonnie's truly breathtaking views of the Hudson River from her twenty-eighth-floor terrace. It was in the middle of a perfect moment, with all of the adults sipping wine alfresco and every child playing happily indoors, that Bella came out and announced that she wanted her game to begin, *now*. Her timing couldn't have been worse, as not one adult on that terrace wanted to do anything but continue to bask in the beautiful skyline, sip their Sauvignon Blanc, and carry on with the conversation. Bonnie tried to keep Bella at bay, first by telling her that we'd do it in twenty minutes. Screams. Then she said we'd start right after the grown-ups had finished their wine. More screams. Multiple attempts to stall the game degenerated into parental begging, yet everything was futile and finally Bonnie relented. 'OK, honey, go and collect the kids and bring them out here and we'll play.' But that didn't go down well either, as Bella was adamant that her game would take place in the living room. There trudged eight parents, diligently but begrudgingly leaving their outdoor para-dise to go and sit in a stuffy living room and indulge a child. There were further problems, which resulted in side conferences between Bonnie and Bella, while all of the other guests sat, waiting in an awkward, silent circle in the living room. The whole time I was wondering what the French would make of the scene, although I had a pretty good idea. I wanted so badly for Bonnie to have the power to say, 'Not now, Bella. I will tell you when the time is right.' She definitely needs to summon her inner Chief. Without a doubt, that would be dicey at first, especially when dealing with a child who has been in charge for so long. Daphne, admittedly, is still a work-in-progress but, after enacting a little tough love with Oona, as well as frequently explaining to her in nice terms – I am still American, after all – that I cannot look upon her 24/7, or even 12/7, nor do I want her to demand the atten-tion of other grown-ups, I've seen a huge difference. She can wait! When we have evening guests, I've begun letting the girls stay up later and participate, as long as they can conduct themselves as part of the group and not insist on becoming the centre of the scene. When they regress, they are sent to bed. Daphne still doesn't make it very long before too many demands earn her a walk down the long, lonesome hallway towards her bed, but her older sister has got to the point where she can stay up until she grows weary and asks to go to sleep.

Here's a little smidgeon from an email response about kids at social functions that I received from an ex-pat who has lived on the west coast of France for decades – you might remember her from the previous chapter:

Children are never left out of anything. There are never dinner parties or festivities like weddings where children are not invited. They sit at the table with the grown-ups and eat the grown-up food with a knife and fork (soup, salad, all kinds of stinky cheese . . .) and they enjoy it! Adults treat them with respect and they are loved and cherished by everyone, but they are made to be obedient. Also, another adult wouldn't hesitate about reprimanding someone else's child. They get to stay up very late on special holidays like Christmas and New Year's Eve and often just lie down and sleep if tired. I honestly don't remember seeing a child having a temper tantrum here.

Don't waste your energy on jealousy – it won't do you any good. Be inspired!

That last sentence was written for myself as much as anyone else. It's hard not to turn a little green when French people keep telling me they 'don't remember' the last time they saw a child have a major-league fit. A land without tantrums sounds like fiction to me – or maybe a bath salts advertisement touting supreme relaxation – and I wouldn't believe it if I hadn't heard it from any less than ten French sources. Just off the top of my head, I can list a bevy of Daphne's tantrums from the past twenty-four hours:

– yesterday afternoon she was inconsolable because the tip of her pen 'wasn't bent right' (although she speaks wonderfully, I never figured out what she meant);
– major wobbly because we had run out of bubbles for the bathtub;
– last night – approximately eight minutes of meltdown because she couldn't 'deal' with her blanket;
– a thirty-minute, *very* tearful and loud search party for her favourite tiara this morning, soon followed by . . .
– hysterics over a failed internet connection and thus no video games on PBSkids.com.

The French parenting site enfants-ados seems to have read Dolto's book, posting as they did these '4 Easy Tips to Avoiding a Tantrum':

1 Être clair et fermes sur les principales règles.

2 Rester serein face aux pleurs de l'enfant.

3 Apprendre à l'enfant à savoir attendre.

4 Apprendre à l'enfant à respecter également vos exigences.

Or, in other words (with further elaboration translated by yours truly):

1 Be clear about and firm on the main rules.

   It is important that parents establish *un-bendable rules* for their children such as, for example, remaining seated and buckled in the car seat, holding the parent's hand while crossing the road, going to bed at an established hour, *sitting correctly at the table . . .* rules that differ from one family to another according to the standards of each but that must be firm.

2 Remain calm in the face of your child's tears.

   It is important that parents *attempt to understand whether or not the child is crying for a justified reason and that they know how to detect a tantrum*. If such is the case (that is, the kid is throwing a tantrum), the adult *must absolutely ignore the child*.
   Often, in fact, the child is throwing a tantrum to get attention, to make you change your mind, or to make you give in.

3 Teach your child to wait.

Waiting helps the child to better accept frustration and to learn to be patient. A child must
know that he cannot always have immediate
gratification.
    Waiting does not hinder a child's psychological
development; rather, it contributes to its
reinforcement.

4 Teach your child to respect your needs, too.

Even if it is true that children matter more than
anything else, *it is important not to lose your
own parental authority*. (You are the Chief!)
    A child must learn that you cannot constantly
be at her side, cannot always play with her . . . *It
is important that she knows that you [the
parents] are people and, as such, you need time
for yourselves, for your life as a couple* . . . once
again it is common sense that must be applied.

Before discovering the French way, I had come to accept
that Daphne would launch into a full-on McEnroe at a
moment's notice because she knew that she could, and
that there was a good chance she'd get oodles of sympathy
to boot. However, the Chief (me, dammit!) has been
devoted to rehabilitation. I kicked myself that we were in
this leaky boat to begin with, but *c'est la vie* – I resolved
to fix it.

My plan: I implemented the Dolto-inspired 'Easy Tips' (although they have never sounded too easy to me); more on my results shortly. The truth is, *kids are much tougher than we think*. They aren't going to wilt or have under-developed self-esteem if we say 'no', enforce a punishment, or turn up (in some cases, turn on) the Strict-o-Meter. Dolto uses the term 'symbolic castration' to describe the vexation a child experiences when he or she is given restrictions. She maintained that this figurative snipping is necessary for them to learn to control their desires and impulses. Clearly, my Daphne hasn't spent enough time with the scarily named theories of Dr Dolto. I never thought I'd look fondly on anything involving castration, especially in relation to my children, but it is clear that we could use a dose of this metaphorical stuff. Dolto does not advocate being a tyrant just for the hell of it. She wrote (in French, so I've translated):

> If being strict means forbidding what is dangerous, then yes, be strict – but with compassion and always while respecting the child, who is an adult in progress. We must take the responsibility upon ourselves to restrict certain things because they are psychologically or physically dangerous. If we parents are not strict . . . our children will be forced to regress and censor themselves, or at least try to. There is nothing more debilitating for a child; he wastes all his energy in the effort . . . If we are strict, our children may be furious, but they will conserve their energy . . .

Before I became the Chief, I'd often think about how much energy my kids and I would burn up debating *everything*. I feel like I've had some version of the following argument with Oona at least 2,829 times:

'Honey, get your   feet off the coffee table.'

'But Mom! They like it up there. Feet can feel, you know.'

'Not the right kind of feelings, but nice try.'

'OK, I'll just keep my feet up there for one minute.'

'No, Honey. Take your feet down now.'

'But sometimes I see Daddy put his feet up on here. Daddy even lets me.'

'Take your feet down!'

'And at Sophie's house they're even allowed to stand on the table. Can I do that, then?'

'No. Put your feet down.'

'I'll put on my slippers. Then my feet won't be on the table.'

'For God's sake! Please take your feet down. I don't like to see feet on the table!'

'But I do, Mom. I like them up there.'

'Take your feet off the table right now, or else I'm going to have to think of a consequence.'

'You are a mean mom!'

I am so not a mean mom – by this point in our *conversation*, the kid's feet have been stinking up my table for over five minutes. A true Chief would forbid such foot follies. Riffing off Dolto, the French clinical psychologist Nathalie Rocailleux writes about how important it is not only to lay down the rules for children, especially between the ages of eighteen months and four years old, but also to 'explain to the child the reason for the limits'. This way, kids will 'trust the adult's words and come to understand authority as necessary and as a source of security'. I have a couple of great reasons why I don't want feet on the coffee table (oh, and I should remember to explain these reasons to my husband too). First of all, people eat from there. Call me old-fashioned, but it's kind of nasty to have foot funk, or even the memory of it, anywhere near an eating space, no matter how stinky the cheese itself is on it. Secondly, it's bad manners. Manners are *huge* in France, as I'll discuss later. Right now, I'll just say that manners are good, and a healthy understanding of etiquette leads to better behaviour all round. I have heard it said, and now have found, that strong *structure*, *and ritual* for that matter, not only helps, but actually *creates discipline*. If bedtime always occurs at 8 p.m., without all of the waffling and bargaining I know goes on in many American homes, then children will come to accept it as a given and not create a stink every night when it's time to hit the sack. In our house, we'd disintegrated into the habit of announcing bedtime about twenty minutes before our target time because a long negotiation had become inevitable. If I forget to make the announcement, the girls get less sleep. That's not right.

Rocailleux also points out that adults should set rules that are reasonable – not tyrannical or based purely on their own desires – but that are for everyone's good. She adds that the adult must apply the rule equally to everyone. OK, new rule: no feet on tables. (No exceptions, darling husband.)

I had a problem with giving in to my kids, which is a big, big problem, as it turns out. So many times have I told them 'only one show' (streamed from the internet – at least I've improved things a little by cutting cable TV), and then relented when they sweetly beg for a second episode. Part of the trouble is those cute little faces, which have so much power when used correctly to manipulate me, but other factors that have contributed to my frequent caving-in are: (1) another twenty-five minutes of peace and quiet can be irresistible, and (2) they are so happy and lovey-dovey when I relent – 'You are the best mom in the omniverse!'

Unfortunately, this led us to the point where they do not really hear what I say the first time, knowing that there's a good chance I'll crumble (sound familiar, bedtime?). The French parents I've been squatting with lately would never buckle, no matter how adorable the pressure: 'Catrine – *Don't Back Down!* You will not have so many arguments if you stick to your first word.' So true. In the short time I've upped my hard-assery quotient, I've seen real results. I was so proud when my girls each had a friend over recently. I had given all the kids half of a confectionery treat, and there was one more left in the box. Oona had the bright idea of cutting the last one into fourths. It was reasonable, I guess, but since I'd already set the limit at a half as I knew we were attending a party later in the day, which was certain to add to the treat tally, I crushed her tiny dream. You know what? It felt good. One of the wee visitors, however, had clearly not been exposed to the French: 'Oh, come on! It's just another bite, really. I know my mom wouldn't mind. Please! I am the guest, after all.' There were so many things wrong with her behaviour that I had to take a deep breath, but before I could begin to explain things to her, I heard my own little *cherie* answer for me, 'Don't even try it. Begging doesn't work on my mom. Let's go play.' Score one for the Chief!

This Chief does not always win so decisively, though, so don't be discouraged if change is not instantaneous once you have gone French with your little charges (case in point: Daphne and her tantrums). I've found it very helpful to keep such French wisdom at the ready, but mine has been a deep hole to dig out of so, at least at first, I developed my own little spin on things. Also, transforming my lovable urchins into the little saints I saw in France will take time. Meanwhile, I find comfort in the small victories. For instance, take the advice I've been given from more than a few French parents: *Que le châtiment conviène au crime*. Or, 'Let the punishment fit the crime.'

On the first day of my kids' new summer camp, I succeeded in this – but perhaps the voltage of the punishment was not up to French standards. I arose already nervous about the transition, and then I had the added concern that my little Daphne had gone to sleep late the night before – *quelle horror*, I know. So, I spent my morning fretting over how she would do at camp. Of course, she woke up on the grumpy side. The kid needs her sleep, and if she doesn't get it she tends to resemble a miniature Frankie Boyle: funny, sure, but mostly just mean. As she does every morning, Daphne went to the refrigerator to inspect what I had put in her lunch (very unFrench of me to allow this and even to open her packed lunch up for discussion, by the way). Turns out, a baggie with five little chocolate crackers was an unacceptable sweet. I was already on eggshells with the kid (again, unFrench), so I took Daphne into the kitchen to procure a more suitable lunchtime treat. That went fine, and I *thought* we were doing well. About ten minutes later, Oona sought me out to break the news. Clearly miffed, she bellowed, 'Why does Daphne get a bag of chocolate cookies for breakfast?' More than usual, I was wary of the tinderbox of Daphne's emotions I was handling, and I was also trying to get out of the house in time for the kids to catch the camp bus. The last thing I wanted to have to do at that moment was to have to give her the French treatment for such a transgression. And yet, she ate cookies for breakfast! I had to do something. Deep down, I knew that the answer was to take the other, previously approved, treat out of her lunch. But I just could not face it. She had been so happy with her choice, and I knew taking it away would result in a major meltdown. Given all of these circumstances (and especially the fact that if they missed the bus, I would have to take the girls to my workplace for the day), the old me would have just blown it off with a, 'Daphne, that was wrong. Never do it again! Now let's go.' But I'm in recovery. On the hoof, I came up with a punishment that (almost) fit the crime.

Three Tic Tacs. I took away three Tic Tacs. It might not seem like much, but it was all that was left in her coveted pack that was given to her a couple weeks ago by her aunt. Her freak-out was minimal, we made the bus, and – perhaps most importantly – I had done something! Next time, I'll go full-French on her, provided we aren't running against the clock.

The whole dessert for breakfast fiasco brings up another little area where we American parents might be straying far from the mark. We are a land of free spirits and original thinkers. This is great, but let's be reasonable. I see kids at my local playground tripping all the time because they insist on wearing their shoes on the opposite feet or, even worse, wearing shoes that are multiple sizes too big: 'Oh, he just has a mind of his own and loves to wear his big sister's Vans trainers.' The subtext: 'We don't want to stifle his creativity.' I grew up with New Wave and punk music styles, not to mention the American sit-com *Punky Brewster*, so I can get behind some zany footwear, but I've got to take a page out of the French book when it comes to kids: *don't be afraid of right and wrong*. I know parents here in the States who are so worried about suffocating their children's budding inner artists that their kids are living in a bizarro world where anything goes. It is important to remember that kids are, until about the age of seven, relatively irrational. As parents, our job is not just to give them a good sense of morals, but also to teach them how to do things correctly – from getting dressed to eating properly, to respecting adults – and everything in between. My little cousin used to like to pretend he was a dog. It was in this role that his mother had the most luck getting him to eat any vegetables, so she would often feed him the more *challenging* dinners via a bowl on the ground. She rationalized further by telling us 'how *imaginative*' he was. Now, however, at five and a half, he's still not big on the ol' knife and fork. I like to imagine him at his first power lunch, howling at the moon, rib-eye remains splattered on his face. For now the family can't eat out in a restaurant without some kind of shame, given the manners displayed at the table.

French table manners will get their due ink soon enough, but let me explain a bit about what is expected of French children in other areas of etiquette. I was floored when I went to France and was repeatedly greeted with immediate, alternate, side cheek kisses by the children of friends, acquaintances, even interview subjects I had just met. Never was a child allowed to look past me or, God forbid, scowl at the American stranger. And nine times out of ten, they didn't need a reminder from their vigilant parents to carry out these warm salutations.

The whole of French society is very polite, and it is still considered very rude for a person of any age to enter (*Bonjour!*) or leave (*Bonne journée!*) a store in France without hailing the shopkeeper. The amount of '*mercis*' and '*pardonnez-mois*' going down at any given time is staggering, as well. It is gorgeous to behold.

Witnessing this, of course, conjured up images of my own kids back in the States. For instance, they have both lived in the same apartment since birth, yet they still habitually shrink from – or, at best, ignore – certain older neighbours. It is always humiliating – and we can do better. When I began this adventure, I simply insisted on a change with this speech (or one very similar): 'Guys, children must *always* show respect for grown-ups – especially those that they know, like our neighbours or Mommy and Daddy's friends. We have a new rule, which is that you are required to say hello to a grown-up that you know, especially when they greet you first. It will make you, me and the grown-ups happy. If I see that you are not doing this, there will be a punishment.'

What happens when they don't comply? So far I haven't had to invent the punishment, but I'll never forget the long faces of a couple of French kids I know here in the States when I saw them in the neighbourhood one autumn afternoon. When I asked why they looked *soooo* sad, I learned that their mother had taken away their Halloween candy for three weeks because they failed to say hello to an elderly woman from the neighbourhood. I mean – that's harsh. But I can only assume that they didn't do it again.

Manners and respect are consummately linked for the French, so I tried to go deep with the respect at the same time – especially with Oona, who has a habit of condescending to adults. Two words, darling: not French. But it can be tricky, like when she *informed* the cigarette-wielding grandfather of one of her friends, 'You know, smoking is very bad. It will make you die. You should not do it any more.' I was caught somewhere between horror that my kid was attempting to reprimand a human at least fifteen times her age and relief that I had got the message across about nicotine. Still, it is not her place to speak like this to a grown-up, especially an elderly one. This has also come out in Oona's blossoming environmentalism. When she sees someone leave rubbish behind, her instinct is to yell 'Don't litter!' I do not want to squelch her green streak or give her the impression that it is, indeed, OK to trash the planet, so I have instructed her – especially if the offender is old enough to be her parent – to temper her criticisms. Lately, her favoured response is, 'Excuse me. You left something on the floor. I'll pick it up if you won't.' It still seems a little cheeky to me – but she's right, people shouldn't drop litter.

With all this theoretical respect flying around for other grown-ups, it was time that Mac and I got in on the action as well. Being treated like a servant and a doormat had become very tiresome. In our brave new Frenchified world, Oona and Daphne are sent to their room if they criticize Mac or me. Same goes if they denounce something we have done for them – like prepared a dish that is not to their liking or combed their hair in a detestable (in their estimation) manner. They can express an aversion – as they both did for tonight's chicken and dumplings – but it must be done with courtesy. In the place of previous reactions like, 'This is gross! I won't eat it!', I hear more civil rejections such as, 'I'm sorry. I tasted it and I really don't like, it.' Tonight, Oona even threw in, 'Poor

Mommy. You worked so hard . . .' Maybe next we'll tackle sincerity.

French parents are also very creative in their insistence on good manners. To a child who dared slouch at the table, I heard one French mother explain via severe snap, 'You act as though you don't appreciate your vertebral column. You are not a worm – don't sit like one or your bones will soften and you will have to slide your way around town.' They are firm in their ways, but not without humour.

Being a Chief with unbendable rules helps enormously with getting kids to behave, and there is another thing that I've learned from my international pals: *more stuff is not the answer*. I'd fallen into a habit with my own kids that involved *a lot* of rewards. Somewhere, I had read something about always focusing on the positive and not constantly pointing out bad behaviour. Quaint in theory, but kids are smart and, in practice, I had really just put a huge target on myself that read. 'Manipulate me.' We got to the point where my girls thought that if they made it through a long subway ride or a dinner out without causing some sort of havoc, they were, ergo, entitled to a prize. I'll never forget when Oona and Daphne sat through *Horton Hears a Who!* (a *kids'* movie – not my first choice, if you catch my drift) and asked me what they could pick out for being so *good* in the cinema. This was one of those pivotal moments when I knew things had to change. In France, the children are civil because they have been taught, from the earliest age, that this is the only option. It's so refreshing to be with French families wherein children can come into a room of conversing adults and not have to disrupt the scene. They often just sit down and listen. If they have something to contribute, they do, but most often with respect for the communal conversation. In the few instances I have witnessed of children trying to stir things up and demand attention without a worthy contribution, they have been either told to leave the room (and they did) or they were simply picked up and removed. Each time, the parent returned moments later as if nothing had happened. No long negotiations on the other side of the curtain. No excuses or apologies upon re-entry. Just back to the business of hanging out. But where did the offending child go? Usually to his or her bedroom, although I've seen kids put in a bathroom, even a little cupboard and, of course, *Le Coin* (the corner) for such outbursts. French parents manage to cultivate a healthy dose of fear in their children, which I am sure is why I never once saw a French kid go bananas when they were sent away for acting inappropriately. Not long ago you could not have convinced me that any amount of fear a child directed towards its parents could be healthy, but that was then. I am not advocating that we want kids who tremble in our wakes, but I know that in order to achieve respect, a little bit of consternation is not just a good thing, it's *necessary*.

I will admit, this is sometimes achieved in France through a little technique called corporal punishment. It is not uncommon over there to see a child receive a smack for acting up. Not all French parents spank their kids, of course. In fact, of all of the folks I interviewed formally, only two admitted to ever thwacking their children to keep them in line, and both claimed it was a one-off thing. However, the eyes do not deceive. I saw kids in France thumped (never too hard, by the way) on the Metro, on a merry-go-round, on the streets, in stores . . . you name it. For the record, this is one instance where I disagree with the French style. Not only does hitting take terror too far, but in the States it is also a really bad policy for other reasons. Spanking is taboo here, and any kid who gets a swat is going to feel really, really, really bad about it. They will likely feel that because they are so beyond redemption, their parent had to resort to *that*. In France, it's normal enough not to carry the same psychological weight. Most French parents are simply working from the same model their parents had used with them (not to excuse them). These days in the States, kids are practically born with the number of the child protection services imprinted on their fontanelles, as well. It's just not cool. Command respect with your voice and attitude, but leave the paddle on the Continent, *s'il vous plaît*.

Now, back to Daphne's progress under the tutelage of my French pals. Did I mention the size of the ditch we had to dig ourselves out of? I've a hunch that the above-mentioned tips to avoiding tantrums are a great deal easier when applied to a subject who has not grown accustomed to daily conniptions from years of practice. In other words, Daphne is a tough case. Again, I would just like to suggest to anyone with very small children – get French sooner rather than later! Now, for the rest of us, I am happy to report that, although it's been no cake-walk, we are on the mend. For the past two months, I've been nothing but French with Daphne – the days of wimpy Tic Tac corrections are over. I wanted to do this right, but I also wanted to avoid humiliation, so I timed the beginning of tantrum boot camp with the beginning of summer, and the idea that many of our friends and neighbours would be out of town and thus not around to witness the inevitable carnage. The most difficult, and yet also rewarding, suggestion to implement has been teaching my daughter to wait. I see her little body trembling, wanting so badly to erupt. These days, as often as not there is no detonation – which is indeed major progress for all concerned. I've found it so effective in diminishing freak-outs that sometimes I'll have my kids wait just to bulk up their 'waiting' muscles. Whereas a year ago I might have thought this sounded cruel and unnecessary, I truly believe that it's good for them.

In these parts, helicopter parents are only being replaced with lawnmower parents (look it up, it's a real condition), who are equally at the ready to remove any impediment to their child's joy. Sadly, their omnipresence is an obstacle in itself, as we'll see a bit later.

Just as my kids do with their dinners – miserably swallowing down every last green bean before getting to the grilled cheese and frozen mango – here I've saved my best discoveries for last. Recall that my introduction to the world of French parenting was the adage 'If there is no blood, don't get up.' When I first heard it I thought it was funny, and at the time I was thrilled because I really didn't want to leave *my* friends and attend to Daphne's demands for me. Now, as I get deeper into the mind of a French parent, I see that there is much more to it. Teaching children to be proficient in waiting is good for everyone – even the neighbours, especially the ones who live near the lift in our building.

I have had many talks with my girls recently about the new, unbreakable quality of my rules, as well. For instance, crying when an internet connection is lost – and, with it, the show in progress – now results in the computer being put away. It was hard on all of us at first – believe me, once you've tasted freedom doled out in delicious twenty-two-minute intervals, it is tough to give that up. However, now they know this dictum, and when the signal fails they have just about learned to look at me pleadingly (like there's anything I can do . . .?), sometimes fighting tears, but the point is that they are fighting their emotions and not me. It is not wise to pick a fight with the Chief.

The beauty of the French approach, of course, is that you do not find French parents screaming at their kids across the park, restaurant, department store or wherever, to keep them in line. Their emphasis on the good of society is not only their inspiration in raising well-mannered kids, it's also the reason they don't allow themselves to get riled up in public. It's like double discipline. One French mom, Helene, let me in on her secret for when she wants to yell at her child in a public setting. 'You whisper. Bring your child very close to you and whisper in his ear quietly and calmly what it is he is doing wrong and why he must behave. I even do this at home sometimes because the whispering seems to really get the child's attention.' On the other hand, when things get even a little bit out of hand, I've seen French parents pull out the ever-effective (though so cruel) weapon of humiliation to combat unruly behaviour. For the French parent, this comes with the added *benefit* of proving to everyone that they are doing their job as a good parent and teaching proper behaviour. But, ugh – I could never say 'you are acting the imbecile' to my girls, especially in front of a playground full of kids (the offence of the little 'imbecile' was interrupting his mom, by the way). Publicly disgracing a kid is a tad too sadistic for my taste, and I'll leave that one in France.

Still, I love a good little tip. Another one Helene gave me was her 'no eye-contact secret'. With American in-laws from Iowa, Helene has spent more than a few summer hours in playgrounds in the American heartland, and she told me:

[I will] never get used to the way the moms [in the States] rush to comfort their kids, sometimes before the kids are even having trouble. If I see my child fall down or have a problem in the playground, my way is to not look him in the eye right after. If he knows I saw him fall, he might cry just for the comfort. If he comes to me crying, he's usually truly hurt. And that really does not happen very much. But some of these kids in Des Moines are always crying and I don't even know why.

With so much laying down of the law, I was struck with the response received when I asked French parents what they do – and what was done to them – for issues of lesser offence (though American obsessions) such as thumb-sucking, bedwetting, and even nail-biting. The prevailing attitude that I detected was to let it be. This is the land of laissez-faire, after all. 'These things will work themselves out, Catherine,' I was told. As the mother of a very dedicated thumb-sucker, I have, with the help of the World Wide Web, worked myself into heart palpitations trying to figure out what to do about her habit. Visions of misshaped jaw bones, thumb sores, untamed tongues, collapsing nostrils, low SAT scores and other related horrors haunt my brain. In expressing these fears to a Parisian mother of two thumb-suckers, she replied: 'You worry about her test scores? We will have to fix some teeth, this is true. But we cannot cut off their little thumbs. I do not worry about these things. They are just children, after all.' *Just children* – isn't that what we often use to excuse sweeping tantrums, finicky eating and straight-up brattiness? Interesting, yes, but also ironic. My child was chastised by her dentist, her teachers . . . sigh . . . and even me, for doing something she's unable to help, yet when she deliberately acted like a twit, I often looked the other way and rationalized that it was all part of being a kid. This French attitude also goes a long way to explaining why I saw so many children in France over the age of two using soothers. It's not a high-calibre battle for them – not nearly as important as controlling themselves in public.

Ah, but what about a child who hits others? Surely this would stump the French? One overseas mom said to me, 'If he hits, then he is not allowed to play with the other kids. If he does it a lot, I say just go find another child who also hits and put them together. See how he likes it then. That is what my sister did with her son.' I'm not persuaded that this is the best approach, but it is useful in illustrating a different, less overwrought angle than, say, turning to therapy, which I've seen several friends enlist for their physical little hotheads. It also goes along with what Jeanne, another French mom I encountered, declared as her parenting philosophy: 'This too shall pass.' Only it didn't sound at all New Agey – if anything it sounded quite the opposite: bored, pragmatic, unimpressed with life's lumps.

On the subject of excusing bad behaviour, I was not surprised to find that the whole business of birth order – as in, 'Daphne is rambunctious like every second child, that explains it' – is not a big topic of conversation in French parenting circles. Did we will it into existence as with the Terrible Twos?

Picking battles is a recurring theme I have noticed with French parents. They don't negotiate, but they also don't turn everything into an issue. And *voila*! – their kids follow suit.

For years, I've heard tales of these magical European babies who are all potty trained well before they turn two. Sitting down for coffee with a French mother of five sons, I asked her how this was possible. Lord knows I tried to free up my kids from the nappies early on, but it never really stuck (until three and a half, for one of them):

> Well, I do just what my mom did. When the babies are about nine months old, you do not put nappies on them after their meals. Then, in a little while (the same hour every day), you put them on their little pots. I was working so I had the babysitter do it for the boys. Well, except for my last boy, who really just liked to wear nappies. So, he wore them. I didn't make a big deal about it. The others were never doing their poops in their nappies any more, and then it was easy to teach them the pipi.

I suppose that even if I had known this technique when my girls were babies, they wouldn't have been French enough to sit still on the potty for any extended period of time – score another point for obedience. Still, had I been a bit more laissez-faire in my attitude, my poor little daughter (I refuse to say which) wouldn't have had such a hard time with it. If I never have to hear the words 'stool retention' again, that'll be too soon. But, apparently, according to my books and blogs, this happened because of all the potty-training pressure I heaped on to my girl.

OK, so the bottom line is be strict, very strict – but not too strict on certain things. Got it?! I'm getting there.

French Discipline - The Abridged Version

1 **Do not forget that you are the Chief** (*N'oubliez pas que vous êtes le chef!*). Since when do two-year-olds get to call the shots? This isn't healthy for anyone in the family, yet the practice seems to be rampant.

2 **Structure/ritual creates discipline** (*La structure crée la discipline*). There are reams of research out there showing that kids tend to thrive when they have structure and routine in their lives. Routines help teach kids how to constructively control themselves and their environments. And they definitely cut down on power struggles: their enforcement becomes expected, and the parent doesn't have to feel like some evil, haphazard ogre . . .

3 **Children are tougher than you think** (*Les enfants sont plus robustes qu'ils apparaissent*). Children don't 'deserve' a say in every disagreement. It simplifies things for everyone if they understand the meaning of NO! It's not going to hurt them to respect and trust parental decisions.

4 **Let the punishment fit the crime** (*Que le châtiment conviène au crime*). Little kids are not clairvoyant, and their limited exposure to the

ways of the world must be kept in mind when disciplining. It's important that, when possible, the punishment be related to the offence. For example, if they throw a toy, take away the toy.

5 **Do not back down** *(Tiens le coup)*. When you make a rule, you must stick to it. If people thought they only had a 50 per cent chance of being arrested for illegal activity, I am sure that more would try it. If you make a threat, follow through. Too many parents don't, and kids end up interpreting their threats as 'I have a few chances before they'll do anything.' Endless warnings are far from effective.

6 **Do not be afraid of right and wrong** *(N'ayons pas peur du bon et du mal)*. The fact is, children are not rational. It's your job to teach them not just morality, which is certainly important, but also, quite simply, the right way to do things. You aren't stifling their creativity when you insist they wear their shoes on the correct feet for a long walk, for instance!

7 **More stuff is not the answer** *(Ne nourissons pas la rapacité)*. The outcome of giving children treats and toys when they demand them is that they will just demand them more. A little self-control (across the board) goes a long way.

8 **If there is no blood, don't get up** *(Si il n'y a pas de sang, pas la peine de se lever)*. Kids are capable

of going from fine to completely off the handle in seemingly no time. They are also just as able to go back to fine in record time, so don't tire yourself out getting up for every scream.

Reel Talk – Parenting Tips Au French Cinema

The French have a long and remarkable history when it comes to film production. A list of some of the country's top directors reads like a Masters of Cinema syllabus: Godard, Truffaut, Renoir, Chabrol, Rohmer, and on and on. While the nation's greatest cinematic gift must be the French New Wave, there is also much to be learned and loved when it comes to Franco films featuring relationships between parents or teachers (or mayors!) and children. The films below all contain excellent parenting insights and epiphanies – and they go down easy, with great production values! Now get out that bag of popcorn – or, better yet, warm your croissant – and dim the lights.

Ponette (1996) This heart-twisting film shows just how independent and resilient kids can be – or have to be, as the little girl at the centre of the story must carry on when her mom dies. Stock up on tissues – it's worth it!

Small Change (1976) Known as *Pocket Money* in France, this is François Truffaut at his mischievous best, along with a cast of incredibly clever and cute kids. One teacher offers a line revealing how the French refuse to sugar-coat the world for children: 'Life is hard, but it's wonderful.' A good lesson, *non*?

To Be and To Have (2002) If this documentary about a very rural school, the thirteen children in one class, and an acutely inspirational teacher doesn't warm your heart, then . . . your heart is really, really cold. See a doctor or something!

L'âge de raison (2010) Remember, the age of reason starts over there at seven years old. So watch it with your six-year-old! The kid in question writes in a letter: 'Dear Me, Today I'm seven years old and I am writing you this letter to help you remember the promises that I've made during the Age of Reason . . .' I mean – swoon.

Les enfants du Marais (1999) This film, on the other hand, portrays three badly behaved kids and serves as a reminder that not all French children are tiny miracles. Then again, it takes place in 1918, so we can assume that if there's a remake, the kids' parts will be rewritten and sweetened.

My Father's Glory (1990) You know how a lot of French films feature impossibly cute kids gallivanting across gorgeous country vistas while lit perfectly by award-winning cinematographers? This is one of those. Prepare to want to move to turn-of-the-century Provence and raise your kids there.

The Chorus (2004) Another familiar trope in Franco film-making is the stern but loving teacher who arrives at a new school and goes about improving the lives of troubled students. *The Chorus* is built around that kind of story. And a neat trick: how did the director ever communicate what an outburst is to his young actors? They must have looked at him like he was crazy or speaking another language.

Mon père, ma mère, mes frères et mes sœurs (1999) The heroine of this film is a single mother who has three kids by three different fathers. In the States this character might be called a 'degenerate suck on society'. But in France she's considered a free spirit. And she's a good mother who is living the life she wants – so I salute her.

Le Papillon (2002) A kind-hearted old man, a gentle, precocious kid, a hunt for a rare butterfly – what more could you want? Well, Jean-Paul Belmondo, sure, but other than him? Not a thing.

Our Children Will Accuse Us (2008) In this documentary, a mayor fights to ensure that kids only get organic food in schools in southern France. You read that right. Told you they take food seriously.

4

Homme, Femme, Enfants or How Boundaries Saved My Sanity

There is a certain limit to the number of times parents should have to say to their child, 'Don't lick my nose' or, 'Keep your hands off of my butt'. I'd love to have set the maximum at one, but we passed that marker long, long ago. It was kind of sweet when my girls were breastfeeding infants and would obliviously explore the terrain of my chest, neck, face, you name it, but I should have carved out a real line beneath the underwire at some point. Hugs and kisses are great (always – please don't stop that, darlings), but what I've experienced was quite often akin to groping. I would tell myself it was normal – they are just curious and attached to me. All good, right?

But, in truth, I didn't want my body to be open for action, day and night. From the very beginning, *le corps* of a French mother is fiercely protected, whether through a limit on the breastfeeding, the kibosh on children in their parents' bed, or the all-important message that Mommy's skirt is exquisite and one shouldn't stand on it, especially when she's in it. (Note: French moms almost never sport *les sweatpants*.) Until very recently, my kids would often sit on me, hang on me, swing from me. There were no barriers – as though they were under the impression that my existence on this planet was solely for them. Imagine.

'Don't give everything to the baby. Especially, remember that your breasts are for your husband.' I love this quote, a little bit of *wisdom* imparted to a French friend by her doctor after the birth of her first child. I love this quote for what it suggests – and for how hilarious it must seem to nearly every American mom.

For my husband – ha! That's the last person I was thinking of when my kids were born. The only time I imagined him in the same setting as a pair of knockers was when I wished he could have grown a pair of his own to help out with the seemingly endless breastfeeding that I'd once so willingly signed up for. But this cautionary lesson is one that French women learn from their environment immediately after, or maybe even before, they give birth.

Over here, we are warned that our children will have low IQs, suffer horrendous allergies, become obese, and essentially come up short in every endeavour they attempt, unless they want to be serial-killing shut-ins, if we don't nurse for roughly fifteen years. Over there, the French are cautioned that they will lose their sex lives, their figures, and even their marriages if they hand it all over to the new, precious little sycophant in the family. I have been inhaling my own pro-breastfeeding air here for a long time, so I'm not about to go full French in my attitude, but there is a certain amount of irony in the fact that French offspring rank much higher when it comes to education – and let's not get started (yet) on the whole obesity thing (in both the USA *and* the UK).

And the way their kids eat, I doubt many French schools are serving up spelt crackers as a wheat alternative because of widespread wheat sensitivity. Suffice to say, for the French, keeping boundaries firmly in place starts from birth.

What about that husband and his claim on my rack, you ask? At the risk of sounding like the main cover feature of *Cosmopolitan*, there's something to this. When you surrender everything to your adorable spawn, it can become difficult to find the path back to your own sexy scene. The grip of obsession is fierce and, as we've established, the trend *du jour* for American parents is to completely fixate on their kids – at the expense of practically everything else in their lives. Not long ago, I ran into a mom from the neighbourhood who declared she was 'sleepwalking', having spent nearly three hours on the internet the previous night searching for seamless socks for her four-year-old. 'She really has a thing about any socks with seams at the toe and there is always a conniption when she has to put shoes on. It's scary how much I love flip-flops these days. Anyway, Brad is a little steamed because he says I've ruined our Saturday now. I guess I am a little out of it.'

Probably didn't do a whole lot for their Friday night, either. And I have a hunch that that kid could learn to tolerate a hint of thread near her toenails. The screwiest bit is that only a few weeks ago, the same mom had complained to me that her husband was so consumed with selecting the safest car booster seat for this same sock-challenged daughter that he spent hours creating an Excel spreadsheet comparing different models. Clearly, this couple are in desperate need of a date.

Now, back to *les boobs*. Once, in a conversation about breastfeeding with a group of French women, I got a lot of strange – horrified, really – looks when it came to the question, 'How long did you nurse?' In this group of five women, only one besides me had gone as long as six months: 'I'd decided to take a year off work and the time just ran away from me,' she explained, almost as though she was apologizing. The others all packed it – them – in by three months. It's not surprising that, in the Western world, the French rank the lowest in terms of number of months allotted to breastfeeding. I'd nursed Oona for fifteen months and Daphne for eighteen. 'Eighteen? Eighteen? *Incroyable*. Impossible. You must mean eight,' they exclaimed over there.

I then explained to these completely stupefied madames, and now it sounded like *I* was apologizing, that I'd always intended to wean Daphne at fifteen months so that things would be even between my kids. I harboured a fear that *if* I nursed one longer than the other, and then the one that got extended boob-time ended up being a piano prodigy or teenage open-heart surgeon or something, early-weaner would blame me for playing favourites. But when Daphne's fifteen-month birthday rolled around, she would have none of it and I failed to seal the deal for another three months. This made absolutely no sense to my French companions, and I had a sensation – one that I was becoming well acquainted with in my interviews with French parents – that I was slightly deranged when it came to certain aspects of parenting. I could not tell if, at that point, they were more puzzled by the length of time that I nursed or by the amount of thought and worry I put into this hypothetical situation of an adult daughter feeling that she did not get her fair share of breast milk. You can imagine why I refrained from describing my many unsuccessful attempts to shut off the valve with Daph, which included a solo trip across the country for three days with the express purpose of 'drying up', various replacement incentives like little puffed fruity things and new stuffed toys if she cooperated, and many other ineffectual schemes. Alas, she was stronger than I was – a bit of a pattern when I look back through the history of our battles. I still recall the force with which she brought me to the floor and pulled up my shirt when I returned from my transcontinental experiment. I simultaneously laughed at my toddler's determination and mourned my failure to reclaim my body after over a year of suckling. While the French don't really hesitate, I worried that if Daphne was still so attached to nursing, then clearly she *needed* it. No, I did not admit any of this to the French. They most certainly would not have understood. More than that, they would have been aghast and thought less of me: *Why is this baby making the decisions?*

Why, indeed.

The other side of this is that many French moms also don't understand how completely heartbreaking and devastating it is for many American moms who *fail* to get the hang of nursing, or are faced with a kid who doesn't take to the tit. The pressure to be the perfect nurser is not there in France. French women are much more likely to be ostracized for nursing past three months than for not. I have heard stories of *rebel* French moms who nurse in secret to escape inevitable stares and aggressive tsk-tsking – and unsolicited advice and warnings about how they are ruining their lives and the lives of everyone they love. The French can certainly be harsh.

I'll never forget the complete anguish my good American friend went through when she had a difficult time breastfeeding. She wanted to be 'the best mom she could be' – so she tried and tried, but it just didn't take. Before she threw in the burp cloth, however, she invited two representatives from La Leche League to her apartment for a consultation. The meeting resulted in my friend leaking only more tears and feeling like a miserable failure. Breast milk still wasn't flowing and the consultants, insisting that she had to find a way if she was 'serious' about the health of her child, had managed to upset her even more. Before they left, they admonished her for the size of her bed. According to the leaguers, my friend's double – and not queen size – sleeping accommodations were restricting the baby's ability to nurse properly.

This guilt pile dumped on my bottle-feeding friend was completely unnecessary – and totally unFrench. (Although make no mistake, the French have no problem offering their opinions. They just wouldn't knock the bottle.) Another pal of mine, who begrudgingly nursed her child well past his second birthday, lamented the 'damned if you do, damned if you don't' feeling that is so bound up in this issue. It's as though we have to choose between doing what we might think is best for our babies and what is best for womankind. *Zut alors*! I vote that we respect each mom's personal decisions and not judge one another so harshly.

Well, to a point. There may actually be a time that is *too long* to nurse. I remember witnessing a somewhat disturbing scene on a plane a couple of years ago. A child, I'm guessing nearly four years old, was still on the mommy meal plan. He was begging his mother for a little teat, and this poor mom, who had clearly discussed nursing in public with this kid, was frantically trying to fend him off in forced whispers: 'Not now. You know the rules.' Finally, the little boy desperately exclaimed, 'Well, can I at least just see them?' In France, it's largely regarded as obscene – and damn close to child abuse – to nurse longer than one year. Good thing we weren't on Air France that day.

In this area, French women have a very public advocate, of sorts. And get this: she's a philosopher! Yep, over there it's still possible to be a living, valued – even popular – philosopher. After coming across one of the current French faves, Elisabeth Badinter, I understood a little better why French women are so different from Americans in their breastfeeding habits. For years, the feminist Badinter has been attempting to safeguard the role of women in French society and the workforce, which has improved dramatically in the last few generations. *La philosophe* is read so widely that French women could often find her book, *Le conflit: la femme et la mère*, for sale in their local supermarket after its publication in early 2010. The title translates to 'The Conflict: The Wife and the Mother'. Badinter is on a crusade to save French women from losing all the ground they have gained socially and professionally over the years. Although, by and large, French mothers breastfeed for a far shorter time than in the States or the UK, Badinter is still wary of a little trend she sees developing towards 'natural' parenting in her native land. Not only does she vilify the pressure to breastfeed, but she has got her sights set on the ever encroaching burden to provide homemade baby food and cloth nappies, all of which she fears will tether women to their children and their homes. She's like a modern-day Simone de Beauvoir.

Part of me – the American part – thinks that Badinter sounds paranoid, overly bitter and a little bit scary. But another part wishes we had our own version of this feisty feminist here. I didn't want to nurse for eighteen months – that much I remember for sure. Yet I didn't have the balls (pun intended – ha?) to end it. Ladies – don't let the pressure and guilt keep you in the same *bateau*. You've got a life too, so be strong if that is what you want.

Now, for a little bit of questionable advice. While most

French mothers don't need to pull out the heavy artillery to unlatch their babes, as two- and three-month-olds aren't capable of too much resistance, I still managed to elicit from a collection of Frenchies a few tips for weaning particularly stubborn cases (please note, I do not endorse the ones with asterisks):

- *Cover the nipple and half-inch area of breast which surrounds it with colourful body paint to confuse and discourage the child
- *Sprinkle some pepper or rub garlic on the nipple as a deterrent
- Feed babies/toddlers before they are too tired or hungry and do not need to nurse for comfort
- Do not hesitate to give them a soother in place of the breast

This difference in focus between the French and Americans is truly fascinating. I've had a female French visitor in my room who announced, out of the blue: 'If you get rid of that big bed and get maybe the double size, you will make love more often with your husband.' The advice haunted me for weeks because I love my big bed. But then, so do my kids.

Probably the most effective way that French parents have managed to cut down on the breastfeeding is by keeping *ze leetle* babies out of their bed. Here in the States, the words 'sleep training' are as controversial and brimming with emotion as 'breastfeeding'. Or 'dog fighting'. In France, there's no heated debate about how to put babies to sleep. Known as *le rituel du coucher* (the bedtime routine), – *it's just how it's done*. With baby Oona, I had been reading Dr Michel Cohen's parenting book and I ended up acting surprisingly French on this score. When she was about four months old, Mac and I commenced with 'Operation Cold Turkey/Wild Turkey', in which, after having spent every single previous night in our bed, we placed our precious bundle in the crib at 7.45 p.m. and resolved not to get her until at least 6 o'clock the next morning. The Wild Turkey bourbon was to help our resolve. I think I only got down about a thimbleful on the first night because I was so focused on and horrified by the shrieks of my infant. (Mac didn't have the same problem.) By the third night, however, the whisky was going down smoothly – well, as smoothly as Wild Turkey can go down – and Oona slept for eleven hours straight. Note: I didn't touch the whisky until after she had nursed, so don't get any ideas. Oona has maintained her sleeping talent ever since.

Daphne, as is often the case, is a different story. Maybe it is because I knew that she was most likely to be my last baby and thus didn't even try to start the process until she was over six months old (by the way, Dr Cohen advocates starting at two months, and the Wild Turkey was our idea, not his), or maybe it is because I was so exhausted from holding her all day that I didn't have the energy to resist or endure Daphne's night-time wails, but I was not very French in trying to get her out of my bed. And man, did I suffer. If I could have had that kid sleeping in her own bed by a respectable age (even before she was four), I might have had a chance at a decent bedtime routine. As it was, it took years and years before my husband and I could reclaim our California King mattress.

Thinking back to a dinner party I went to in France, I realize how much I could have gained from drawing a few lines. When I first arrived at the dinner, I was somewhat disheartened to see that my hosts' children were still awake. These kids are quite adorable and, of course, well behaved. But at two and five years old, I assumed there would be some serious surrender in the adult ranks. In my brain, their little pyjamaed presence translated to the eventual loss of at least one of their parents – relegated to a protracted 'bedtime routine'. There's no other kind, right? Wrong. At bedtime in this *maison Française*, the kids were assisted with brushing their teeth, and after that they obediently took to their beds. I swear, both parents were in and out in under ten minutes. It was like witchcraft, and I so wanted into the coven. During dinner parties at our place, more than once I have disappeared to put the kids down and not emerged for over two hours – just as the gathering was breaking up. Talk about depressing.

Trying to be more French, I recently put my foot down and cut the nightly song roster from eight lullabies – eight! – to two (one pick per kid). Oh, and we now have a twelve-minute limit on books, which must be started by 8 p.m. or book time is forfeited. I thought I was truly learning, and I have managed to cut our routine down considerably . . . but our nightly ritual is merely French-flavoured and not the real deal. Then again, I'm doing better than my friend here in the States who admitted that she and her husband both bring their phones into their children's room at bedtime so that they can talk via text – as the kids refuse to fall asleep without them in the room.

Back in France, after the safe, swift and utterly seamless return of my friends to the table, I pumped these two magicians for information: 'The baby is in her crib, but she knows that even if she cries it will not do any good, so why should she bother?'

Gulp of wine.

'Sometimes, not very often, she does anyway, but we cannot get her. Then she would do it all the time. And the older one understands that this is not his time. This is the moment, every night, for grown-ups to be alone – even without guests he knows he is not welcome.'

Gulp.

Not welcome may seem a little callous. Perhaps something was lost in translation. But no, I don't think so. From a French viewpoint, it is not harsh at all. In fact, I wish I heard about putting out the 'Not Welcome' mat quite a while ago. In France, this is simply the arrangement that everyone has been taught. Had I only introduced a similar concept early on, Mac and I wouldn't feel like we won the lottery when we managed to get a few nighttime hours alone. Yet in many a French home, a little solitary wine-drinking time, among other things, for the parents is a recognized right. And dang if those French kids didn't go right to sleep. I'm obsessed with sleep and the countless studies on its relationship between everything from SAT scores to obesity. (Hey, breast-milk, this sounds familiar!) Still, even on those rare occasions that I get my kids into bed by 8 p.m., there is always at least half an hour of consultation and adjustment that goes on. Anything from a simple request for water (both of my girls) to an urgent question about mammals (Oona) to the cryptic desire for a different set of jim-jams (Daphne) to the critical need of a leg massage (Daphne) to the sudden realization that I had not sung the right songs (Daphne) – ah hell, the 'Daphne' list could go on for pages. When we nip this bedtime thing in the bud, French-style – and we will! – my girls could clock up to four extra hours of sleep a week, which they are going to need when I get French on their schooling. Those are four hours that I could spend hanging out with my husband. *Gagnant–Gagnant*! (That doesn't really have the same ring as Win–Win!, though, does it?)

Basically, at a fixed hour, among my French pals it seems to average around 8.30 p.m. but this varies a bit – especially among different ages, little French children go to their beds. They don't get up because that's *just not the way it's done*. I'm tempted to get that phrase tattooed on my forearm for inspiration, by the way. Who's with me?

I'm sure I wanted the same for my nights but I clearly did not get the message across to the team. In fact, I routinely allowed Daphne into our bed when she habitually woke up two hours after (finally) nodding off. Here are a few of her greatest hits in her brief history of bed-swapping:

'But, Mommy, your bed is softer than mine. It's not fair!'

'I think my bed keeps me awake.'

'Mommy, you'll be hurting my heart if you don't let me sleep with you.'

'My brain feels better in here.'

Clearly – and I should know because I regularly ended up in Daphne's bed and sharing with that kid, California King or no California King, and it is like sleeping with a rheumatic hyena, only more difficult – these complaints were all bogus. Her bed is delightful. But it is hers, and mine is mine, dammit. Daphne's bed has a Care Bear comforter and stuffed animals in it. Mine has my husband. So – I was weak. Don't make the same mistake. If you are a committed co-sleeper, God love you – but if not, don't give an inch because they'll take you for miles.

Children have their designated spots in the French home for slumber – and that's not the only place they have their designated spot. Most definitely, in France kids are kids and not little adults who get to participate in rule making. In my neck of the woods (and my sister's on the other coast, and my friend's smack in the middle of the States) we've replaced our children with little dictators who call the shots. We actually used to lovingly refer to Daphne as 'Little Muss', derived from Mussolini, due to her ability to always get what she wanted through volume and coercion. Cute?

She had ways of making us all kowtow to her will. I fear that my arm is permanently deformed from twisting it up and back so as to hold her hand while I was lying on the floor next to her bed – per her tiny command. French kids, by contrast, have rights – children's rights. One of these is the right to learn from their parents how to be civil. The all-important boundaries are clearly drawn. So much so that if you wander the streets of Paris (on any weekday save Wednesdays, when there is no school), it will look as though children are banned from city streets. This, of course, isn't true – I'm pretty sure, though never say never over there – but they are few and far between from about 8.30 a.m. and 4.00 p.m. An American friend of mine living in Paris alleges that you can find kids in the Seventh Arrondissement during these hours, but I wasn't able to confirm her claim. It is rather ritzy over there in Seven, so perhaps it's the nanny nerve centre. I kept thinking about the town of Vulgaria in the film *Chitty Chitty Bang Bang*, eerily absent of children who are all captive in a drippy, underground cave, and found myself half-looking for a special French version of the child-catcher, with his creepy moustache and a beret in place of the top hat. Not to worry, though, all the little French kids are just safely tucked away at school, at *maternelles* (early school for young students) or government-subsidized daycare centres for the babies. A huge number of women go back to work after having kids in France. The French government just makes it so flippin' easy. I know of many American moms who quit their jobs to stay home with their kids, not because they necessarily wanted to, but because it made more financial sense than paying the high price of childcare. But there's nothing to be gained from wallowing in things we can't change.

When it comes to thinking about how individuals fit into society, Americans couldn't be more different from the French. The reason it is OK to reprimand someone else's kid in France (unless, God help you, it is a wee American tourist) is because the French truly believe that it takes a village to raise a child, whereas in the States we are all about rejoicing in the individual. I'll never forget being on a train out in Bonneville, France, when I discovered – two and a half hours into the ride – that there was a two-year-old and a six-year-old seated three rows behind me. I had just awoken from a delightful afternoon nap when I saw them carefully and quietly making their way down the aisle with a man who, I presume, was their father. The trio was whispering in deference to the many sleeping passengers (again, *sleep is a huge priority* for the French), even though it was about 3.00 p.m. As they passed me, I was momentarily returned to the dream I'd just been immersed in. Most of it had vanished, but I distinctly remembered a lot of whispering. Could it have been that these kids were able to speak softly for two and a half hours and their cute little whispers had infiltrated my dream? I am a very light sleeper. This was a revelation, and I've since been trying to engender the same kind of regard for the needs of society in my kids. As it is, I can barely keep them quiet on Saturday morning to let their father *sleep in* until 8 a.m., so this is no small chore.

'It's not all about you' – that's a new phrase in my repertoire that I would not have dared use a year ago.

The author Raymonde Carroll tackles what this means in relation to bringing up children in *Cultural Misunderstandings: The French-American Experience*:

> When I raise my child in the French style, in a sense what I am doing is clearing a patch of ground, pulling out the weeds, cutting, planting, and so on, in order to make a beautiful garden which will be in perfect harmony with the other gardens. This means that I have in mind a clear idea of the results I want to obtain, and of what I must do to obtain them. My only difficulty will lie in the nature of the soil, given that I apply myself regularly to the task, that is. But when I raise my child American-style, it is almost as if I were planting a seed in the ground without knowing for sure what type of seed it was. I must devote myself to giving it food, air, space, light, a supporting stake if necessary, care, water – in short, all that the seed needs to develop as best it can.

This is a fantastic analogy, and it has really stuck with me. Poignantly, one of my favourite spots for child-watching is Les Jardins du Luxembourg on the Left Bank of Paris (also great for crêpe eating, and then crêpe-regret – but that's another story). There is a beautiful, old, rather rickety and soulful carousel in the middle of the park. One afternoon I witnessed the perfect distillation of extreme American/French parenting. It was about 3.00 p.m., so very few kids were out. That afternoon there were only two riders on the carousel, one American and one French (very French, as it turned out). They were both about four or five years old. This fabulous carousel, built in the nineteenth century by Charles Garnier, the architect of the Paris Opera House, is also famous for the brass ring game in which *les petits* riders are given a little wand, and every time they go around they try to lance a brass ring held by the carousel operator. By the way, it seems as though they've been using the same sticks and brass rings since the very first ride. It is old-school fun at its finest. The American parents were very attentive, and every time their little prince came around the bend they would cheer something along the lines of 'You can get it, Toby!' or 'You nailed that one!' Or, inevitably: 'Good job, buddy!'

At one point, Toby tried to spit on the riderless horse next to him; his doting parents did not cheer then, nor did they reprimand him. Many French people have told me that in their estimation, when a child misbehaves, the stain is on the parent. That explains why the other couple at the carousel, a pair of French grandparents, were flinging dagger glances towards Toby's parents. When they were not looking completely disgusted with the Americans, this older French couple spoke quietly to each other and appeared to have only one interaction with their little charge during the ride. Namely, *la grand-mère* stood up to swat him on the hand for becoming (in her estimation, because I didn't notice any horseplay) unruly. I might have audibly guffawed. Not very polite, I know – but it felt as though this comic, nearly slapstick, performance was staged for my benefit.

On the one hand, especially from having spent so much time in France at that point, I was annoyed by the American parents' over-enthusiasm and I felt a little bad for Toby, who maybe even started spitting to shift his parents' focus from the damn brass ring. And my heart also went out to the French kid, who got thumped in the middle of a merry-go-round ride for no discernible reason. It dawned on me that perhaps the little French fella suffered the slap because his granny couldn't punish the Yankee spitter, yet she felt she had to do *something*. It was all too much for her ordered, rule-abiding, respectful French senses.

This short ride underscored yet again just how differently from the French we Americans approach parenting. In fact, I've asked and asked, but I have yet to find a word in French that translates to 'parenting'. There is certainly no French word that takes on the same strain, strength and stress. In a branch of Fnac (a leading French cultural products group) I popped into when I was in France, I am almost certain that the section housing philosophy books for young readers – like tweens – was bigger than the sector (a table, really) devoted to childrearing. When it comes to a concept of 'parenting' as we know it, the French are more likely to favour a word like *l'éducation*. It explains a lot, as the French are training their children to make it in an adult world, while American and British parents are always looking for a way to survive in our children's world.

For me, life in the 'Adult World' was fugitive at best post-childbirth. Starting the moment I first became a mother (and ending recently – *merci* French ways!), such a place was a taunting Elysium, often within sight but usually out of reach. I've always been haunted by a feeling I experienced the first Friday afternoon following my return to work after Oona was born. Rushing to the subway to get home to *my baaaaaby*, sporting clogs and a breast pump briefcase, I was slowed down by the traffic lights at a busy intersection. Waiting there for the lights to change, it hit me: never again would I be rushing off to meet friends for Friday night happy hour after work. The thought was so sombre and distressing that those sensible shoes would not move, and I stood there like a big sack being jostled by a regular mob of New Yorkers at rush hour – me silently and sadly taking leave of my old self, the image of a margarita fading away. Soon enough, my anguish transformed into guilt (a sensation now in regular rotation) for even indulging such tormented thoughts while my helpless infant was waiting at home. What a troll! Here I was pissing away sacred time with my baby thinking about myself. I then sprinted (as best one can in wooden-soled footwear) the last two blocks to my subway stop.

This memory marks the beginning of some chemical shift in my brain, where it was determined that I had to spend as much time as possible with my kids. I did. And I don't recommend it.

While in France, I went out dancing with my friend Sylvie. The fact that Sylvie, the mother of a ten-month-old, could go to a disco at the weekend was impressive enough to me, but more awe-inspiring was that her husband, Karim, had taken their daughter with him to his Moroccan hometown for two weeks to visit his family. Two weeks! I kept asking her if she was freaking out and feeling heartbroken without her baby. 'No, not really. Do you think I should be?'

Well, no. But my American self could not fathom any other way.

I've spent so much time and soul-sapping energy caught up in the drama with my daughters and our collective torture over this guilt-riddled dynamic. I am certainly not the only American mom who suffers because of it. In fact, journalist Judith Warner wrote an excellent book, *Perfect Madness*, about the root of this problem, which she terms the 'Mommy Mystique'. My children aren't particularly clingy when measured next to their American peers, but compared to French children they're like Glenn Close in *Fatal Attraction*, minus the butcher's knife.

Although I often longed for real time off from Oona and Daphne, I regularly felt too bad about this to leave them. This has affected not only my sanity but also my career, my social life and even my marriage. The first time my husband and I were bold enough to leave the kids for more than a handful of hours was our tenth wedding anniversary. Pretty pathetic when you consider that we'd started having kids five years after we got hitched. We had always talked about spending a week in Paris (my Francophilia rears its beret-topped head), but when the anniversary arrived, we dared only go as far as New Orleans (for about thirty-eight hours – including the flight). Yet, it took enormous effort, which I recently relived by re-reading an email I'd sent to my brother and his wife, Ben and Penny, who stayed with the girls while we were away. I was tempted to include the message, but that would almost double the length of this book. OK, not really – but we are talking many, *many* bullet points. At four and six, my girls were capable of speech – they could have told their minders where to locate extra pants, and I suppose Ben and Penny didn't need to know that the kindergarten teacher gives out stickers. I managed to put together this novella for the babysitters, yet I remember being so pressed for time preparing for our trip that I ended up forgetting my own toiletries. Even more ridiculous – Ben and Penny had lived with us, on and off, for years. Of course, the reason I went into manic mode was that I was utterly plagued with guilt for leaving my babies (who, by the way, were so not babies any longer).

I do have to reveal a little piece of the email in the interests of illustrating what I've managed to overcome with Daphne at bedtime:

2) Bed – As Daphne doesn't nap at school, she's been going to bed by 7.30 (or earlier) and usually sleeping until 7.15. If this happens, she'll be fine. If she goes to bed too late or wakes up too early, I'm afraid that you are screwed. She becomes a raving maniac by the next afternoon. We've been starting bedtime at 7.00ish to get them down by 7.30. Oona will want you to read from a Ramona Book, and Daph will probably pick a stack of other ones. OK, I've mentioned that Daph is impossible, right? Bedtime is the biggest challenge. Lately, I've been working on

leaving the room before they are asleep, so we usually read, get in bed and turn off the lights (and turn on the flower nightlight on the castle bookshelf). I lie on the floor with the 54-inch pillow and the other soft pink one, sing them a song or two, and then the rule is that I stay for 3 minutes (which is usually more like 10 because I get comfortable and don't want to get up). Then I get up and give them 3 kisses and three hugs. If either is already asleep, skip the hugs and kisses. When I leave, I leave the door open. Half of the time, Daphne will come wandering out. If she hasn't napped that day, there's a better chance that she'll conk out immediately. Anyway, she's a pain. If she comes out, do whatever you want. I usually sternly say she has to go back to bed, but if you guys yell at her she's likely to freak out so I'll just leave it up to you.

Here's the really great part – EVERY SINGLE NIGHT (usually between 1 and 3), Daphne makes her way into our room. At that point, I go to Daphne's bed and Daphne sleeps for the rest of the night in our room with Mac. Don't judge us – we are so tired and Daphne is IMPOSSIBLE (see references above). So, you can plan on a little bit of musical beds. On the bright side, Daphne's bed is so comfortable.

Aah, that guilt. It is a scourge to the parents, particularly mothers, of my generation. Like many of my friends, I gave up my full-time job when my first child was six months old and I'd been back to work for four months, because I was sick with worry that I was short-changing my baby by leaving her with a nanny – and in my case the 'nanny' was Ben and Penny. I had heard the refrain 'Why even have a child if you are going to pay someone else to bring it up?' so many times that I began to believe I was a terrible mother for working. Not the highest earner at the time, financially it almost made more sense for me to stay at home than to pay for childcare. For many American women this is not an option – yet they often still suffer a mountain of guilt. Along with my job, I also gave up my gym membership, any need to dry-clean my clothes, and a whole part of my brain that was once reserved for thoughts about things like books and art. There seemed to be no room for that kind of reverie any more with my new mindset, which was now filled with panic about making it to sing-along on time or whether or not I was properly moisturizing Oona's skin.

I'm not sure why I felt such intense pressure to spend all of my time with my kids. In fact, I don't think it's particularly healthy, and I don't want the same for my girls when they are mothers. But everywhere I turned, from the marketers to the mommy blogs, I was bombarded with guilt, and it worked a treat on me. It is truly a joy to be coming out from under this cloud. The new refrain that I have been trying to spread around is 'Why should women have to completely give up their identity just because they decide to have children?'

I do see now why it's easier for a French mom not to endlessly yearn and roil in worry, guilt and boredom, even when they are away from their children for more than a day. At first I thought they possessed a different chemical make-up that instructed them to take time off from the kids – time for careers, holidays, wine, dinners alone with their partner, regular intervals of peace and quiet, and wine (yes, I said wine twice). Once I really got around, I realized it wasn't some fluke brain modulation but rather French society – from French obstetricians to priests (and seemingly everyone in between) – that was sending the message. Doubtless, the memo translated into English is *très* different in content. Where the French are told that it is a duty to the family to devote ample time to the marriage and *not* become overpowered by the lives of their children, I believed that my sole duty – purpose – was to give everything to my kids.

It's no wonder that this idea found its way into my psyche; if you tune in, which most of us do when we become pregnant, you will hear the constant humming of parental sacrifice. New and expectant mothers take in a single phrase ad nauseam: your baby deserves the best! Indeed, it must be the first line that marketers are taught to melt the minds of their parental prey; it's applied to selling everything from changing tables to nappies, to air purifiers (and the aforementioned wipe warmers). Google it and you'll see that there's hardly any item from baby-land that isn't sold with this guilt-inducing maxim.

But really, does my child *deserve the best* changing table? My first baby got it (because I'm a sucker), but I gave it away before having a second and then discovered that a mat on the bed was just as effective, and a whole lot easier. In retrospect, I'm sure that a safe and service-able table would have been just fine as well. I'll give in with the air purifier, especially if a kid has asthma, but a nappy bag? The best onesie? The best nightlight? Merchandisers want to sell their wares, so it's not surprising they've gone down the guilt route (let's remember the cord blood controversy from earlier). Combined with all the other messages new parents receive in the States, there should be some kind of compassionate supervision of the practice of messing with *les nouveaux* parents.

My parenting pals in France tell me that they do not feel beset in the same way. There's not a lot I can do about how we are marketed to, but I can remind you that you aren't a bad parent if you don't get 'the best!' organic flannel and towel set ever made out of hemp by the mountain women of Transylvania.

Am I starting to sound like Elisabeth Badinter or what? No, I suppose she would pronounce it 'emp'.

Most of the time, worry is a waste of energy. For a while there, I was beating myself up for not making the time to teach Oona to tie her shoelaces. I worried that she would be mocked or embarrassed by her inability, but remembering my own struggle with the laces, I was waiting for the right time and a sufficient stockpile of patience and strength to begin with Oona. Then, one day I overheard her proudly telling Mac that her teacher had anointed her 'the class shoe-tier', and whenever kids needed help, they were sent to Oona. Apparently, while I was wallowing in the shame of being a bad mom, she'd taught herself how to tie laces. There is a lesson here.

I'll admit, I was pretty pumped up with the prospect of re-entering the Adult World as part of my Franco-parenting enterprise. Why, sure I'll go out to dinner more, spend regular time alone with my husband and friends, shop by myself, read grown-up books – all in the name of promoting a healthy home life. In reality, it took some genuine, often uncomfortable, effort. Letting go of the guilt, which had been as constant a companion as my children themselves, is rather tricky. The adjustment for my family to a model with a mother who pursues her own interests and has a social life turned out to be the most complicated for yours truly. Initially, Oona and Daphne were outraged with the semi-regular Saturday-night baby-sitter. And they were miffed that I started reading novels at the playground instead of watching their every little stunt. But they caught on rather fast – *it's just the way things are done*. My husband loves it because we have more to talk about than what Oona ate for lunch or who in Daphne's class can ride a two-wheeled bike. For me, however, there is a constant game of childrearing Whac-a-Mole in progress with a form of angst that so many American moms are attacked with (Whac-a-Neurosis?). I'll stretch out with that Pulitzer-prize-winning novel and then feel guilty – like I should be making playdough or researching summer camps. That is when I summon to mind the French design; legions of *mères et pères* who don't spend their days hustling to make their kids' lives perfect in every way. What is even better, it seems to be good for the kids. That is, if you consider a serious decrease in the frazzle factor a good thing.

I learned a lot through some international playground hopping. The scene at the jungle gyms in France is much different from what we have got going here in the States – namely, a pack of hyper-engaged parents trolling behind their little charges to ensure their safety, or simply to be there as head cheerleader, digital camera whipped this way and that in place of pom-poms. In France, you are more likely to see kids playing and grown-ups sitting on the benches, either reading or chatting to each other. There appears to be no compulsion on the parents' part to monitor every move, trick and potential misstep their children might make.

When I went to France last year I was at first a little concerned about my plan to observe playgrounds. Wouldn't the parents and nannies be put off, creeped out even, by the childless lady on the bench? I have no problem figuring out which kid belongs to whom in the States, because if the parent or caregiver isn't shadowing their offspring everywhere, then the kid is constantly screaming 'Look at me!' 'Did you see how good I did?' 'Watch me do it again!' 'Play Monster!' I suppose if the French discerned I did not have a child at the playground they might have thought I was odd, but they had no way of knowing I was unattached. For all they knew, my kid was at the top of the play structure, happily cavorting with theirs. It is not that they are negligent, but rather there is a different perception of the presence of danger in France – the French impression being that it doesn't lurk everywhere.

With this in mind, I've been trying to modulate my own levels of paranoia. Another game of Whac-a-Mole here. I've begun to worry – how ironic – that my own parenting anxieties were detrimentally affecting the girls. Like those times last summer when Oona refused to go outside because she was afraid she had already had too much sun exposure. These should not be the concerns of a six-year-old. There was no mystery about where she got this: I'm a sunblock fiend.

Note to self: *modulate paranoia*.

This reminded me of when I was pregnant for the first time and learned I was having a girl. Mac and I were trying to wrap our heads around our future and found ourselves talking about the children of our friends and, specifically, how it freaked us out that the current generation of little kids seemed so comfortable using the word 'vagina' when describing anatomy. It seemed so clinical and grown-up. We decided to give our kids more kid-like vocabulary. I suggested we go with 'water-hose', the blanket term for all genitalia that my parents had us use while growing up – and now that I think about it, it's possible they still use it. Mac was not convinced. One day we were talking about it with a good friend, who also happens to be a social worker, and she insisted that we *absolutely* had to teach our child (as yet unborn) the proper, scientific terminology because if, God forbid, she was ever abused and interviewed by police or a psychologist, they could not proceed with an investigation if her testimony was not reliable. She even proposed we teach the world 'vulva'. I was immediately persuaded, and my girls are both perfectly comfortable in their anatomical speak (more so than me, I suspect). When I related this story to a French mother years later, she threw her arms up and laughed: 'My God, we are different! If a French child ever said the word "vagin" to a policeman, he would probably think she was being abused at home. No, for the little ones, we say *kiki* and *zizi*.'

I'm not so hung up on what language my kids are using, but I have thought a lot about this instinct to assume the worst possible outcome and work from this point. We just might end up with a generation of jellyfish.

I am trying very hard to be less anxious and compulsive with my kids. This is very French (and thus can be rewarded with a chocolate croissant if you, like me, swing that way).

Of course, the French have their own anxieties and sometimes act compulsively, but those behaviours are generally not their visceral first reaction when it comes to the parenting life. While on a walk with a French father of three, I was schooled on the problem.

You must know, Catherine, kids cannot be satisfied. I see these parents exhausting themselves trying to do all sorts of things to make the children smile and be popular, but these children need to learn things for themselves, too. And they cannot do this if those parents keep doing it for them. No matter what you give them they will want more. It's in their nature. This applies to toys and sweets, but also certainly for attention.

It is not so easy back home to shut off the attention tap, but my husband and I have definitely slowed the outpouring. The girls still often beg us to watch each playground antic, usually on the monkey bars, and we will watch a couple of cool tricks, but there's a limit. Here's my new, French-inspired reaction: 'I'll watch you do it twice, but then I'm going to sit by the tree and read. Practise your tricks well, and I'll watch for a little bit next time we are at the playground and let you know if you've improved. Don't hurt yourself.' God, how I love reading novels!

If you think this sounds cold and heartless, perhaps a quick look at the benefits of independent play will help. In his book *Pediatric Compliance: A Guide for the Primary Care Physician*, Dr Edward R. Christophersen explains that

> children can be taught independent play skills much like we would teach them anything else . . . When a child is able to entertain himself for long periods of time – we look for 1 to 2 hours of independent play by 4 years of age – there is much less need for discipline.

Oh, there is so much in this that warms my over-taxed cockles, starting with less need for discipline. The fact that these skills can be taught is great news for parents like me. Dr Christophersen points out that most toddlers already have these skills, but that their parents don't take the proper steps to foster them. And, I might add, we even inadvertently stymie them. The more I read from *Pediatric Compliance*, the more surprisingly French Dr Christophersen appears. He goes on to say:

When a child has self-quieting skills and independent play skills, the issue of behavioral compliance becomes much easier. For one thing, when parents rely on discipline to keep a child out of trouble, instead of relying on competing activities the child truly enjoys, the parents must maintain a high level of vigilance. In the long run, it is far easier to encourage the development of self-quieting and independent play skills than it is to monitor a child's every activity.

It is also a lot easier to have a phone conversation, make dinner, or even take a darn shower!

But it gets even better, as Christophersen notes:

Children with well-developed independent play skills derive enjoyment simply from their activities, with no need or expectation of the involvement of others or an external reward. Independent play skills enable children to do long homework assignments, to work in their seats at school, to complete independent projects, to read a long book, and to master a hobby or talent . . . Children with independent play skills usually play better with other children than those who do not.

This puts the whole image of an aloof French parent into a new perspective. When Daphne complains, ten minutes after getting home from school, 'I need you to play with me because I have no one else to play with!', I now employ a new tactic. Or I try, anyway. I promise to play for the *beginning only* and we set the timer for fifteen minutes. When the timer goes off, she's on her own. Lately we've been playing dolls, with her favourite two going on hair-raising escapades throughout the house. When my time is up (thanks, timer!), she usually takes over for both dolls and keeps the game going. She isn't up to carrying on solo for two hours yet, but things are certainly progressing. In fact, it is not uncommon at all for her to just initiate a game without me having to kick things off.

How do you say 'Can I get a woo-woo?' in French?

The French parents I observed seemed to have less time to, say, get down on the floor and build a Lego spaceship with their kids or jump into the bunk-bed fort for a tea party because they were busy doing their own things. This made me a little sad at first glance, but after reading the work of Dr Christophersen I am heartened in my search for a middle ground. There are so many benefits for everyone to having a child who can placate himself. Still, sometimes I really want to join that bunk-bed party. So I do.

What I don't want to do all the time is to sit on the side-lines for tennis lessons, hip-hop dance class, cooking club, sewing circle, and on and on. And yet, my children have grown so accustomed to having me on hand that it's been a hard pattern to break. When I learned what typically goes on in the extracurricular world of a French child, my determination was bolstered. In France, if a child takes up a sport outside of school – which, by the way, is not nearly as popular there as here – parents don't usually hang out for every (or often, *any*) practice. In fact, they rarely go to the weekend game, and it's only for the final match or championships that they will make an appearance. Very few of the parents are on hand rooting until their voices are hoarse and/or fighting with the referees, and yet the kids don't feel neglected. Here in the States it is intensely important to rigorously, and loudly, support our children in all of their endeavours so that they feel encouraged to find 'their thing'. Every few months, we suit up for a different, new undertaking – which requires different, new equipment, different arrangements and brand new registration fees. No wonder we don't have the energy – or spare cash – to go on a date.

The set-up in France is distinct. Wednesday, when there is no school, is the typical day for children to take classes, thus freeing up the weekends for real relaxing – and more sleep. Ducking out of school on Wednesdays is not an option for us in the States, but, inspired by the French, I aimed to sedate the pace of our lives. Again, this was not without its complications.

At the beginning of the year Daphne announced that she wanted to be enrolled in *tap*, *sing* (I assume voice lessons), *moderen* (four-year-old speak for modern dance), and *pottery*. Where did she get such notions? From any number of her little pals who bop around to multiple extracurricular activities each week. As this is not sanctioned French behaviour, I signed my girl up for exactly zero of these classes. Having barely lived through the nightly witching hour of Oona as a spent, over-scheduled kindergartner – one who did ballet, drama and soccer – I was happy at the thought of how this different, more relaxed lifestyle might affect Daphne, who was certainly the more *excitable* of my kids. Bingo! The increasingly unhurried clip to our lives has made everyone happier. We are slowly, slowly becoming a decently oiled machine here, and everything – from homework to bedtime – is rarely wracked with the anguish I formerly thought was just par for the course. Daphne will have opportunities to learn her ball changes and scales in due time.

By the way, in addition to taming little Daphnes, I've a hunch this French priority of traipsing rather than hurtling through life might account for their more domesticated male offspring. American parents of young, practically feral boys often gaze longingly at me with two little, comparatively tranquil girls. I'd estimate that about 40 per cent of the little boys I know have a little extra oomph in them, and that their woeful parents just seem to be waiting it out until the constant urges to jump on other kids mellows out. But damn if that 40 per cent doesn't seem more like 10 per cent in France.

As you can see, the French approach to classes and activities for their kids is certainly less vigorous. Instead of spending all their free time searching for, say, their five-year-old's talent and life passion, the French keep things more open and flexible. For those classes and sports that French children do pursue, their parents are often not part of the experience. I happened to be in France the afternoon that a friend's eight-year-old started a new dance class. This little girl, who is half American, had her heart set on learning hip-hop, but there were no such classes offered to children nearby. *Pas de problème* – she opted for the adult class. Her mom walked her across the busy crossroads to the building where the classes were held because she was still too small to do that alone, but once there, the kid was on her own. She came home and reported that at first the teacher was very sceptical but grew less leery when she caught on quickly, and he had agreed to let her come back the following week. I keep trying to imagine Oona doing something similar, even with me holding her hand and watching the entire class, but it does not compute. I have heard more than one Frenchie argue that by letting children do things on their own, something that they can practise and tell the family about with pride, the kids end up much happier and more confident.

This sounds great in theory, and yet I have still only managed to slip away for one of Oona's tennis classes. At this point, she prefers when we tell her, rather than she tell us, that she's doing really well. No doubt, this is the result of being told throughout her entire life that she is amazing. I fear that she needs endless approbation to do anything vaguely challenging. As you might recall from the carousel scene, French adults do not praise their children with the same frequency and volume as we Americans. Before I committed completely to the French approach, however, I needed to do due diligence to these two divergent approaches and see what the experts make of them.

The result? Point to the French.

At least if you listen to current theorists who claim that

many American kids, who have been lauded at every turn, are suffering the effects of overpraise *and* hollow praise. All of the kudos appears to be putting a damper on the output of effort, as children either believe that they can't do any better or they just don't want to try and risk their perfect standing. But on top of this, kids are pretty smart, and after about the age of seven they become skilled at identifying (locally sourced, farm-raised, turkey) baloney. If the praise is not sincere (I shudder at the memory of telling Oona that her seal drawing was 'stunning' – truth is I initially thought it was a giant tongue licking a UFO), they catch on quickly, and any form of praise thereafter has little meaning. Dang.

Somehow, maybe in part because of Dr Nathaniel Branden and the popularity of his book *The Psychology of Self-Esteem*, we are obsessed with self-esteem in the States. My friend Sandra, who moved from the South of France to Los Angeles when she was thirteen, loves to tell the story of one of her first weeks in American high-school. Her class was engaged in some sort of activity that required them to look in a mirror and tell themselves how important and special they are – listing all of their best attributes. Still in the French mindset, Sandra was utterly confused: 'I thought it was ridiculous and mean-ingless. Why should these nice things mean anything coming from me to me.' I guess Dr Branden hadn't really taken off in France in the same way. This same friend remembers the first time she was given a peanut butter and jelly sandwich for lunch. She genuinely thought someone was playing a joke on her.

Where we might err on the side of overpraise, the French could do with stepping it up a little and to let go of those humiliation tactics. Meet me halfway, France!

It has been exceedingly hard to deprogramme myself from telling my kids how wonderful, bright, beautiful and, yes, perfect they are fifty times a day. Now, I am down to about ten, a good thing as Oona has begun to pick me up on it: 'Are you just saying that because you are my mom and you have to?' This is a difficult question to answer and I wish she had never thought to ask it. It is not easy to help a child improve on something if you have told him or her that they already produce genius-quality work.

It could be that when we fixate only on our children's happiness and never let them feel wretched, or anything close to it, we are just laying the ground for future, adult discomfort because not only will they lack the tools to deal with pain and disappointment on their own, but they will pulse with guilt for not feeling great! All the time! They did, after all, have such amazing (read: martyred) parents.

It is as though contemporary American parents don't know where to draw the line – or even if there should be a line at all. Eileen, a doctor friend of mine, recently told me a story that chilled me to my core and made me realize how slippery this slope can be. Eileen was in the consulting room with a middle-aged female patient. The patient's phone rang and she excused herself, telling Eileen that it was an important call. Eileen then listened to her patient trying to console her nearly thirty-year-old lawyer daughter, who, she could not help but overhearing, had just been reprimanded at her new job at a law firm. The next time Eileen saw this patient, she learned that the lawyer daughter had since been fired from the firm – not because of her poor performance, but because her mother had called the senior partner in the firm, a man she had never met, to rebuke him for admonishing her daughter. Could the signals be clearer? Cut the cord!

That's not easy, of course. I know of what I speak. Not long ago Oona was rejected from a clique of girls in her class, some of whom had previously been close buddies (if that can be said of kindergarteners). One night at bathtime it all came pouring out, the tears slashing into the sudsy water: 'Annabel, Sarah and Evelyn don't ever want to play with me. They just want to play alone. And Annabel called me a nuisance!' Sarah's mother, Megan, is a good friend of mine, and my first instinct was to call a meeting. I was halfway through the sentence, 'Don't worry, Honey. I'll call Megan and we will work this out', when I realized that I wasn't going to do my daughter any favours by having her friends' mothers force them to play with her. Unfortunately, life does have its hard moments – *c'est la guerre* and all that unpleasant jazz.

Oona had grown accustomed to having me, or my husband, solve all of her problems and she wanted, even expected, me to call Megan, but I held strong. It was hard for both of us, yet in the end we both came out a little sturdier. Oona pushed herself to seek out other friends and discovered that the world does not end when things do not work out just as she'd planned. I was able to detach myself just a tad from my beloved daughter's social life (to be honest, it makes me a little queasy to even write that sentence). It all felt very French.

As parents, it's not easy to disentangle our own emotions from those of our children, especially when we have never tried. Parents these days seem to view their children as mini extensions of themselves, and not as independent beings that need to learn how to navigate the world, for better and for worse. We already know what disappointment, pain and fear feel like (I do not know anyone my own age who was reared amid the same protective and indulgent tendencies as we use with our kids) and want to avoid it at all costs for our little lovies. The thing is, our kids *need* to experience these things in order to get along in life. It is healthy. Somehow, when we surrendered everything to those adorable kids, we lost sight of this fact. Whenever the subject of coddling came up in my conversations with French parents, they always pointed out how very important it is *for the children* that parents let them be alone, solve their own problems, and experience – and get over – discomfort. Most certainly, it's important for the parents – and their quality of life – as well.

It is even harder to play critic and certainly disciplinarian if you are always in buddy mode with your kids. Last summer, over lunch with a group of French parents just outside Paris, I found myself talking about the American inclination to be pals with one's child and, fatefully, I used the word 'buddy'. You'd have thought I had let out an enormous fart or disparaged the work of Serge

Gainsbourg based on the combination of eye rolls and giggles that rippled around the table. (For the record, I am not especially flatulent and *J'adore* Serge.) I then learned that in certain French circles, the 'B word' is a point of ridicule.

'Oh, we hear it all the time,' one of my lunch companions lamented, laughing. 'I work with this American and he can't seem to stop with it. Things like, "Come on now, buddy, don't be mad at me because it's time to go. Please, buddy." Buddy! Buddy! Buddy! or, "Way to go, Buddy! You ate your cookie!" and things like that. I want to say to him, "You should try being the father and let the child's friends be the buddies." The poor child cannot do anything without his father buddy, buddy, buddy all over him.'

Another cringe moment for me. I could just hear my own voice from the past echo, usually after a scolding, 'We're buddies, right?' When you think about it, it does sound kind of desperate – not a sentiment that I would necessarily associate with a Chief. The French really make a distinction between the parent and the child – with parents on an elevated level. I can see why we have trouble getting our children to obey. Even worse, we find ourselves constantly bowing to the demands of our kids – why would they think it shouldn't be that way, seeing as we are all just buddies?

Always referring to a child as a buddy must take its toll on the parent's mind as well, and I'm sure this is related to why we feel so wretched leaving our buddies behind when we attempt to go out on a date. Who would leave a good friend screaming, clawing and begging at the door? If we avoid this dynamic from the kid's first day, we will dodge, or at least diminish, the tortuous scenes at the door.

By being truly in charge and not a buddy, I have accomplished a change in the house that has me dizzy with delight. One day, I just stopped and took a good look at my home, a large three-bedroom apartment in Brooklyn with spacious dining and living rooms. Not one of the eight rooms was free of kid chaos and clutter. There was an enormous play kitchen in our living room, a wagon full of toys in the dining room, piles and piles of art supplies in the kitchen, where the walls looked like they belonged to a small art gallery featuring only the scribbles of children. Mini-Mondrians they ain't. Not even the hallways were safe from kiddie trinkets. And I'm not talking things that were left about, but toys that 'belonged' there when they were put away. I also thought back to the dwellings of my French friends, and I realized that it didn't have to be this way. Sure, my children are a huge part of my life – but just as I had learned that they didn't have to completely take over my mental space, I discovered the same applied to my physical turf. In the French model, children generally keep their things in their rooms. The rest of the house is usually free of kiddie litter. This is somewhat flexible, of course, but the big exception is the living room. There are no toys in the living room. The living room is sacred. Children aren't banned, but they certainly are not encouraged to use it as a play or storage room. Adults like to sit on living room couches and, *oui!*, enjoy a bottle of wine with their adult friends. Thrilling, no? It helps that French kids don't usually accumulate the same volume of toys as their American counterparts, but they also are brought up knowing that there is an aspect to their parents' lives that does not revolve around them, and that part of adult life requires its own terrain.

Since my modus operandi in this project is to go rather French with my childrearing, I took the leap not long ago and removed all toys, scooters, colouring books, adorable fake appliances, sporting goods, mediocre and inspired art projects, board games and stuffed animals from the living room. While I was at it, I rearranged the furniture – in fact, I had to because I had so much rediscovered space in there. It felt like Christmas. I beam with mammoth pleasure just thinking about it. Remember, I am not at all a stickler, so a few contraband toys and books do creep back to the coffee table, but these things can be whisked away in under a minute when I want to feel like a grown-up – and not a Toys R Us manager. When a friend commented, not long ago, that 'the living room feels much less stressful' before she had put her finger on the changes, I had to hug her. Victory was mine!

One French mother, whose five sons are now grown up, confessed to me that she wasn't always such a stickler either: 'I am not so strict with this. I used to let them bring their toys in the living room on Sundays. But there was the condition that they had to clean them all out before the weekend was over.'

What a softie.

Last spring I spoke with a twenty-three-year-old from Bordeaux, Noémi, who described the controlled kitchen environment in her home while she was growing up:

There were only two drawers that I was allowed to open in the kitchen. Well, one was not really a drawer, it was our little bread box. And the other was a drawer that had crackers and things like that. I was not permitted to go and open the refrigerator and search around. This was the territory of my mother, and my brother and I had to go to her if we wanted some food. Of course, if my parents were away on vacation, we would search through everything! It was very exciting for us.

I say 'well done' to any mother whose kids get a thrill from opening the fridge door. It actually makes sense that little children not be allowed free rein in the fridge. They are, after all, not the most rational beings when it comes to nutrition. As soon as my kids could manage, they waddled right over to the big white box and went for it. And for some reason, we did not stop them – until now. I've deemed age seven the turning point for fridge freedom. (In France this is considered *l'âge de raison* – the age of reason – where kids are typically awarded more freedom in many aspects of their lives.) I've also been reminding my kids that never, never – never! – when they are guests in another home, should they feel at liberty to examine the contents of their host's fridge. It drives me insane when my kids' friends are so comfortable, or maybe misguided, that they help themselves to ours.

There is a lot to be gained from an inquest into the mind of a typical French parent. Their intense focus on society made me realize that my own intense focus on

Oona's and Daphne's individuality has served as an excuse for some really bad behaviour. Still, I am not thinking about crushing them – just dimming the spotlight a tad. Having carefully scrutinized the French, I have come to view their relationships with their children in a whole new light. They have a way of adoring their kids and making them feel completely loved, but still maintaining an enormously high degree of control. On top of that, French parents do an admirable job of preserving their own identities (and, with it, their sanity). I'm even sleeping better these days, not waking up in the middle of the night nearly as often thinking about whether or not Daphne has clean leggings for school or if I remembered to sign a permission slip. In a strange way, the strictness the French practise with their children early on actually allows everyone involved to relax a little. That is reason enough for me to get as French as I possibly can.

Surprisingly French

French-style parents – and their attitudes – are hiding everywhere around us. While many of them can only be found on television or at the cinema, there are some real-life examples, too. I refer to such non-Franco, unlikely parenting role models as Surprisingly French. The people and characters listed below may not even realize how French they are being – but that's exactly how they are behaving. And their kids are behaving better for it.

This idea all started during my exhaustive efforts to uncover kernels of wisdom related to the ways of French parenting. For instance, as I was first attempting to Frenchify television consumption in my household (and often failing, mind you), I thought I could at least cut down on the rubbish viewing. I had a hunch that my daughters were cultivating much of their deep sighing, hair-flicking sarcastic personas with the help of certain abominable television programmes.

By way of a compromise (I know, I know, so unFrench), I told the kids that we were going to try something new: that's when I rediscovered the Huxtable family from *The Cosby Show*, which was streaming on a subscription internet site. From the kitchen where I was preparing *le repas famille* (see Chapter 5), Bill Huxtable's comforting baritone wafted into the kitchen, and what I heard was *musique* to my ears: 'I am your father! That is all you need to know on the subject.'

So that's why the Huxtable family from *The Cosby Show* top this list. But read on to learn about other stealth 'Frenchies' . . .

Clair and Cliff Huxtable (from The Cosby Show)
The Huxtable kids are, generally, extremely well behaved. At those moments when they stray, Bill comes out with a line like the one above. Perhaps the most parent-abiding of the bunch is Sondra, the oldest daughter in Cosby's fictional family. It's not

surprising, then, that she has a pretty wide Franco-phile streak in her.

Gwyneth Paltrow

Gwynie is on record (yes, with *OK! Magazine*, but still . . .) as saying the following about how she and her husband, Chris Martin from Coldplay, approach parenting: 'We're strict with them to an extent but we also try to be respectful of who they are and work with them when they really want something.' Sounds like a Franco-Anglo-American hybrid to me!

Kids in 'Mob Movies'

I suppose this makes a certain amount of sense: if these kids disrespect their parents, they aren't risking simply being sent to their rooms – they could get whacked! OK, maybe mob parents are a little *too* French, but fire up a few gangster movies anyway, to gather less violent insights on discipline.

Victoria and David Beckham (aka Posh and Becks)

According to the model/television presenter Heidi Klum, this English cross-industry power couple has 'the best behaved kids in the world'. This is coming from the woman who relishes bidding 'auf Wiedersehen' to Project Runway contestants in the *Top Model* television show. So we know she pulls no punches – and suffers no softies.

Rock musician Gene Simmons

If he thinks half as seriously about his dad duties as he once did about man make-up, then it is no wonder former Kiss frontman Gene Simmons has told a celebrity website that he's 'very strict'. And the kids behave well because they're 'not allowed not to'. There's more: 'It's as simple as that. There are no drugs, no booze, and no cigarettes because you're not allowed to. You don't talk potty talk because you're not allowed to. The idea that kids slam the door to their rooms on these television shows is the height of lunacy. All that dribble that Dr Spock was mouthing – he was basically farting through his mouth. Negotiating with your children? Absolutely not.' Rock on, dad dude.

Michelle and Barack Obama

My husband and I didn't just borrow from the Obama parenting handbook – we flat-out ripped it off. After reading that the Obama girls, Sasha and Malia, are not allowed to watch television during the week – only tuning in at weekends – Mac and I instituted the same policy. The results have been fantastic: a considerable reduction in the amount of arguing over when and how much screen time Oona and Daphne are allowed, and a sizeable increase in the number of hours they spend playing creatively. Alone. In their rooms. Thank you, Obamas!

The television character Don Draper

In one episode of *Mad Men*, Don Draper has his daughter, Sally, mix a party cocktail. She's about ten years old in the show. Again, this might be a case of too French, but it was encouraging to think that there was once a time in the States when we didn't pamper our children so very much. That's not to say we should emulate the 1950s parenting style, only that there can be lessons to mine in them there hills. To wit: it's worth remembering that after his break-up with his wife Betty in *Mad Men*, Don didn't marry the awkward-with-kids Faye; instead he shacked up with the nurturing Megan. I think we can all drink to that.

Louis Szekely (aka Louis C. K.)

'I love that kid to pieces, but I wish she was never born.' The American comedian Louis says this of one of his two daughters early on in his television show called *Louie*. And in so doing, the very funny, often filthy-mouthed comedian gave voice to a sentiment every parent has thought but not had the nerve to utter aloud.

Oompa Loompas

For the uninitiated, these are tiny, oddly orange, and work all day making candy in Willy Wonka's Chocolate Factory. Yet, they wrote the de facto French parenting theme song, effectively blaming parents for any kid who is a brat.

Ivanka Trump
From the highly unlikely parenting inspirations department comes this quote from The Daughter of The Donald (aka Donald Trump) on a recent morning talk show: 'It is much harder to be a strict parent and deprive than it is to give. I know that's a challenge I'll be faced with. And it's very hard to raise kids in this climate, in this city, with a good moral compass and a good head on their shoulders. But I think part of it is not allowing them to feel entitled.' Amen, sister! Did I just say that?

My parents
This is probably most surprising to me.

On Trophies and Lies

I once tried to explain to a French friend the American habit of ensuring that every child gets a trophy. This brought on blank stares and lost-in-translation bafflement. 'But why would the one that did not do well get a prize? This makes the winner's prize not so valuable. Why should he even try?' I understand the desire to protect kids from the agony of defeat, but my French pal did have a point. My own kids crave competition, but I'm too afraid to see either of them get crushed. I always end up announcing something like, 'Oona, you are the winner in the short-hair division, and Daphne, you placed first in the category of contestants wearing pink headbands.' Is there a word for 'wimp' in French?

My sister even admitted to me that when she knew her older son would be receiving a trophy for his chess accomplishments (he is a preternaturally talented player), she went out to her nearest thrift-store and picked up a secondhand trophy for her younger, six-year-old as well. When she initially told me about this I thought 'how clever!' – heading a meltdown off at the pass. Now that I view it with the French ethos in mind, it seems rather pathetic. Not that I wouldn't do the exact same thing, were I in that spot.

In the park one day with our French and fabulous – and always kind of amazingly good-smelling – friend Paul, I saw another incarnation of this concept play out. Paul was running around racing with Daphne – and he kept beating her. This makes sense: Paul is thirty-six and Daphne is five. But, unaccustomed to losing, my girl was livid. Paul did not understand and said to her, 'You do not want me to *let* you win, do you?'

Doesn't she? I let her win all the time. I often do whatever it takes to keep my children from feeling anything but joy.

This brings up an important question: is lying bad if it is for a *good* cause? I asked around to see how parents from both worlds viewed the practice. I'm sure you can guess the results. Just in case, here's a breakdown that gets at the (lying) heart of the matter:

The lies we tell our children

American parents:

- The toy store is closed
- We are going out to do work tonight. We have to, although we'd rather stay at home with you
- The whole country ran out of ice cream, but they are making more
- There is a Santa Claus
- I will keep your Halloween candy safe
- I'm sorry. The games on my phone aren't working right now. I'll fix it later for you
- Your picture looks perfect
- I love your outfit
- That's such a creative use of spelling
- I can't be the Monster because my contract explicitly says no Monstering after 3 p.m

French parents:

- There is a Santa Claus
- If you sit like a worm, your bones will soften (Wait, is that true?)

5

Le Repas de Famille or The Family Meal

Now that I have a better idea how the French make the magic happen, I like to think back on the very beginnings of my obsession with French parenting. It's no surprise that food was at the centre of it all.

Let me take you back to my dinner with my French pal Lucie and her family – that fateful night which kicked this whole thing off. Initially, I had suggested lunch to my friend, mother of two and a bona fide Parisian. It didn't seem possible for them to come to Brooklyn from Harlem for dinner – unless we wanted to eat at 5 p.m. Surely she would need to have her kids home by 7 p.m. for baths and their bedtime routine. Lucie, however, did not even flinch at the dinner idea. They would come at 5 p.m. and we would eat at 6.30. I felt a bit guilty imagining her exhausted, strung-out kids arriving back home close to 10 p.m. (the subway commute can be over an hour), but I kept quiet. Although my husband and I had been friends with Lucie and her husband, John, for years, somehow we'd never managed to bring our children together in any meaningful way. By the night of the 'fateful dinner', it was high time for us to hang out together, as Lucie's oldest daughter was already six, we both had four-year-olds, and my youngest was nearly two. At first, the kids were a little shy with one another, but they soon disappeared into Oona and Daphne's room and travelled deep into that wonderful land kids go to when they are having fun (and leaving their parents in peace). I recall my delight on many levels: (1) Lucie's children are bilingual, and they often slip into French without a thought. The possibility that my own kids might pick up a phrase or two made me swoon; (2) In a similar spirit of healthy exposure, Lucie's kids had immediately impressed me with their manners. Perhaps a bit of this could rub off on my little kiddies as well; (3) Almost forty-five minutes had elapsed when I realized I hadn't heard any screaming (except for shrieks of laughter), tattling, or entreaties for snacks or television. Something special was in the air.

Ever since Oona's birth, I'd grown accustomed to socializing under siege – usually with at least one child on my lap. Dinner parties were typically a free-for-all where we tried to eat, see our friends, and survive (not necessarily in that order). I had learned to relate with adults in between 'performances' by my children and/or a friend's kids, while also fulfilling my role as entertainer/chef/handywoman-on-call. With John and Lucie it was wonderful to sit in the living room and enjoy uninterrupted grown-up conversation with wine in hand. I kept mentioning the unbelievable luck we were having with the kids, but John and Lucie did not find it as thrilling. To them, it seemed about as noteworthy as a three-year-old who can walk. When things continued to go smoothly in the kids' room, I got up to put dinner together. I remember hearing Lucie call out something in French, and then her two kids were at my side. Apparently, Lucie had told them it was time to come and help. The weirdest part? They had listened.

The entire evening was filled with these moments of bewilderment. Lucie's children were *so well behaved*, but it was their decorum at the table that really shocked and pleased me. As I did almost every night, guests or not, I had prepared two meals – one for the adults and another made with simpler ingredients and a prayer that it would be tolerable to young palettes. On this particular night, the *kids'* meal was mac-n-cheese, sliced mango and green beans. A sure hit, I thought. The French children, as it turned out, were much more interested in the adult dinner of aubergine tagine with lemon and olives, served over a bed of couscous. In between bites, the six-year-old even asked questions about how to prepare it: 'Do you grill the aubergine first?' Her knowledge and interest in food was incredible. According to my master plan, the children all required only forks with their meal. Upon being seated, however, Lucie's kids both politely requested knives as well. At that moment, I quietly replaced their tatty little plastic forks (decorated, naturally, with hearts and dinosaurs) with the more mature cutlery the adults were using.

Clearly, these kids didn't need to be babied when it came to food. Watching the two French children eating so well at my table (don't even get me started on their table manners!) felt bittersweet. I was, quite sincerely, envious of what Lucie had achieved with their culinary attitudes. The painful thought that I'd been selling my own children short would turn into a surge of inspiration. It can be done! I vowed (once I learn myself) to teach my babies how to love food!

Before love, it seems, comes respect.

And it doesn't come out of nowhere. The French have been cultivating their strong reverence of food for centuries. The French respect and fierce defence of their daily bread (and brie and reduction sauces) is evident in all corners of the culture. For instance, in a recent episode of *Les escapades de Petitrenaud* – a popular French cooking show – the host, upon skilfully completing a ham dish, proclaimed, 'Children, when you eat this Jambon de Paris, Louis XIV has his hand on your shoulder.' How I wish someone, anyone, royalty or otherwise, was guiding me through meals – not to mention operating as a lofty historic chaperone for my kids.

Let's have a look at the approach to lunch in schools in France, which any French parent can do as the bill of fare is posted each Monday for the week. Every day at *l'ecole* the children are offered five courses: hors d'œuvre, salad, main course, cheese plate and dessert. And, there are no menu repeats for over a month. *Time* magazine Paris correspondent Vivienne Walt points out that French schools take it even further by offering dinner suggestions to complement these varied (and very delicious-sounding) lunch menus. Walt, whose own child attends school in France, breaks it down thus: 'The French don't need their First Lady to plant a vegetable garden at the Elysée Palace to encourage good eating habits. They already know the rules: sit down and take your time, because food is serious business.'

I admit that I'm perhaps unnaturally passionate about French school lunches, but I do think they get to the heart (or palm) of the matter. Not long ago, the French government went as far as outlawing school *and college* cafeterias from serving ketchup (except, ironically, with french fries), in an effort to encourage healthy eating. The underlying message here is that in France they really *care* about their food, a value taught at a very early age. In addition to menu items like 'mâche with smoked duck and fava beans, or greens with smoked salmon and asparagus, followed by guinea fowl with roasted potatoes and carrots and steamed broccoli', students at a school in France's Loire Valley are given 'a choice of ripe, red-throughout strawberries or clafoutis. A pungent washed-rind cheese along with French bread and water' for dessert.*

Am I the only one suddenly feeling a little peckish?

I laughed (in that troubled sort of way when something hits distressfully close to home) when a friend in France recounted to me the first day of kindergarten in Paris for her American colleague's six-year-old. On her way out of the school building after dropping her child off, the mother was handed a brochure that listed the lunch items being

---

* http://www.culinate.com/columns/deborah/french_school_lunch.

served for the week. She started reading it on the Metro, and by the time she reached her stop she was in a panic imagining the reaction of her son, who knew only quesadillas, chicken fingers and nuggets and, of course, peanut butter and jelly as lunch foods. What would he do when they tried to serve him parsnip puree and ratatouille (she figured he'd be OK with the bread and strawberries that were on the list)? He would be traumatized! Like any 'good' mom, she rushed home, made a sandwich with her emergency stash of peanut butter, and raced back to his school with it, presuming she had saved the day for the little boy – only to get an earful from the school administrators, disgusted by her pampering and certain that he would eat what was served when he grew hungry enough. Eventually a détente was reached: the American boy would eat his sandwich with a knife and fork.

The French insist upon decent eating conditions in schools for their children. Often, when I question Oona about the untouched items in her lunchbox at the end of the day, she complains that she ran out of time. In French schools, the students luxuriate over the meals and are allotted about twice as long for lunchtime as they are here in the States. (The French also spend about three times more money on school lunches. Cash well spent, if you ask me.) Moreover, I used to feel relief at the thought that if I ever absent-mindedly forget to put utensils in my kids' lunchboxes, there are sporks aplenty offered in the school cafeteria. That relief feels more like a grudge since I have learned that in French schools food is often served on heated plates, with real (metal) silverware and (glass) glasses. Clearly, food in France is to be revered, and lunchtime seems as if it is actually a component of the educational studies. And why not study and develop the palate? Learning about food, the structure of meals, manners and customs is as important as practically every other subject in school. We eat every day – children should certainly learn to do it right! If my kids had been brought up with that kind of attitude, I doubt they'd want to moon me at the table. (Yes, they have done this. Not proud, mind you. Not proud.)

This might be painful, but it's important, so here goes – witness a chart comparing a week of lunches at an American school in Pittsford, New York, to the menus in a school outside of Paris:

French Lunch	American Lunch
Iceberg lettuce with radishes and vinaigrette	Zweigel's™ hot dog on a roll with tater tots
Grilled fish with lemon	
Stewed carrots	
Emmental cheese	
Apple tart	
White cabbage salad [remoulade]	Tyson™ chicken fingers with rice and gravy
Sautéed chicken with mustard	
Shell pasta	
coulommiers [soft cheese]	
Apple compote	

liver paté and a cornichon hamburger	Double cheeseburger with Fritos™ chips
peas and carrots	
mimolette [Edam-like cheese]	
fruit	

Cucumber salad with herbs	Mozzarella stixs with tomato sauce and garlic pasta noodles
Spiced sausage	
Lentils	
Saint nectaire [cheese]	
floating island [meringue served on custard]	

potato salad	Stuffed crust cheese and pepperoni pizza
filet of fish with creamed celery	
sautéed lima beans	
yogurt	
fruit	

Source: http://idlewords.com/2003/03/french_week_on_school_lunches.htm

The French menu is practically worth a Michelin star. Or two.

Now that I have a better idea of where they are coming from, it makes sense that the United Nations Educational, Scientific and Cultural Organization (UNESCO) deemed 'the gastronomic meal of the French' a World Heritage Treasure in 2010. That puts the French meal in the same category as national wonders such as Stonehenge, the Kremlin and the Great Wall of China. We are talking about people who are really proud of their food.

If food and dining are like a class in school, then French parents can be thought to be deeply involved in the homework. I have learned that dinner is perhaps the most important part in a French family's routine, with considerable time spent together deciding what to cook, preparing the food, setting the table and then, of course, eating. Lucie tells me that, on a daily basis, her children, like most French kids, handle raw eggs and separate whites from yolks, use sharp knives, and throw chopped onions in hot oil. They wear little aprons. They sit on the worktop, next to boiling water. They put food in the oven. They learn how to dip green beans in cold water after cooking so that the beans will not turn grey (I didn't even know that last trick). And they sit down at the dinner table, every day, to have a three-course meal.

The kitchen confidence and genuine absorption in culinary processes that Lucie's kids displayed at my house was no fluke. French kids don't need special utensils, raviolis shaped like hearts and stars, or endless pleading to eat well – it's just what they've been brought up to do. Lucie assures me that her kids eat the same way that she did as a child: 'The only addition to the routine that my mother back in France would not approve of is tofu. But then again, why would a petite, chain-smoking woman who believes allergies are a myth, who will tell you that a meal without cheese is like a beautiful woman who is missing an eye, and for whom vegetarians are no less than heretics, admit such ugly, tasteless little squares to the sacrosanct family meal?'

Point taken. Lucie, however, uses tofu to her advantage, incorporating it as a key ingredient in the 'colour meals' that her children love to contemplate (and eat!). Along with tofu, a 'white' meal might include endives, rice and brie – with an apple for dessert and milk to drink. And for the parents' beverage, a nice, chilled Fumé Blanc will do the trick. Turns out that kids love menu planning. For the 'pink' meal, fresh grapefruit juice is the first thing to come up. 'Salmon!' screams the four-year-old, who would otherwise not eat much fish. Pink pasta (a mixture of tomato sauce and goat cheese provides the perfect hue) and beetroot salad are added to the list, and finally they agree on Lucie's daughter's suggestion of frozen strawberries for dessert. Clearly, this approach to mealtime is more than just a means of giving the body energy. For these 'pink' dinners, Lucie further elicits delight from her kids with 'the ice-cubes in which they find a rose bud'. OK, that might be a bit much for me, but I could certainly stand to jazz things up a little bit and take a lesson from Lucie, who has managed to cultivate a loving relationship between her children and their food.

Until we Frenched things up, dinner at my house bore close to zero resemblance to the meals prepared and served in my friend's home – something I aimed to fix. I'm not really sure how I ended up with such an altered system as, growing up, my parents insisted that my twelve siblings and I report to the kitchen at 5 p.m. sharp for dinner assignments, ate *every* night as a family, waited to be excused, and stuck around to wash up and clear up after the meal.

But times have changed.

Heretofore, when my children ate dinner, no one really needed to set the table because if they were not feeding in the living room (in front of the television where we had struck a bargain – they could watch a show *if* they ate their vegetables), they were at the kitchen table. All meals were served on their favourite plates – the plastic kind with four compartments and cute cartoon characters. I would fill each little alcove with a different comestible and, *voila*, dinner was served. If ketchup was in order, it usually went in one of the little plate compartments. Unlike the Reagan administration, however, I tried not to classify it as a vegetable. Occasionally, Oona would grab a couple of forks, but that was hardly setting the table.

My main concern was making sure they ate something healthy, and thanks to the divided plates they got fruit (generally frozen mangos), protein (either some plain chicken, cheese or luncheon meat), vegetables (spinach or green beans mostly, although asparagus is a recent, unlikely hit), and then the wild card (crackers, dried cranberries, half a piece of toast with hummus – you get the idea). This was a typical night in our house.

Sometimes they'd eat tofu (when doused with enough soya sauce), but more often they'd complain that it was 'too creamy'. The funny thing was that most of my friends with kids were covetous of our dinnertime success. 'They eat so well!' I heard that all the time. 'I can't believe they will eat spinach. Miles thinks that anything green has been dipped in poison.'

As for table manners, we had a long way to go. Here's a peek at a previous dinner at our house. By some strange twist of after-school lunacy, I ended up with a spontaneous crowd: three mothers and six daughters. Armed with a family-sized bag of pre-packaged tortellini and a heap of frozen green beans, I proudly, if perhaps too quickly, threw together a meal for everyone. After a lot of cajoling and corralling, we finally had every kid in the proximity of the table. However, I cannot say with any confidence that they were ever simultaneously seated. At one point I looked around – here's the tally:

- Two girls were sitting at the table, quietly shovelling food into their mouths
- Oona was under the table, instructing me to hand her green beans without looking in her eyes
- My neighbour was seated with her four-year-old daughter on her lap, pleading and trying desperately to slip bites into her child's mouth
- One child was in a pushchair munching away
- Daphne was sitting on the windowsill with her plate on her lap

I tried to console myself with the idea that it was the excitement of eating together that caused the children to riot at dinnertime, but deep down I knew the truth. By and large, in an effort to protect our children's sense of self and to honour their emotions, my generation of

American parents has abdicated the throne. The anarchy in my dining room on tortellini dinner-party night, or practically any night, was the result of a new style of parenting, one in which the children are so used to having a say on everything that they cannot take direction on anything. Please now join me for a moment of silence to honour the French insistence on boundaries – they have made all the difference in my life.

In an effort to better understand our predicament, I surveyed about twenty-five American families with children of various ages regarding their dinnertime activities, and I learned two very important things. First off, I discovered that many of my friends lie about how their children conduct themselves at the table, as well as about what their children eat. I know because I have been in many of these homes at dinnertime, and I have witnessed the truth. I've also learned what I already knew – namely, that it wasn't just me who turns into the circus master of a three-ring show every night at around 6 p.m. Here's a sample of the responses to my question, 'What table manners matter the most to you?' (Enough to make any French parent blanch.)

1   Not throwing milk cups across the kitchen, keeping the screaming to a minimum, and asking to be excused at the end of the meal (which they do, despite often doing the first two items as well)

2   No feet on the table. Torsos on the table are frowned upon as well. No throwing food, no

screaming, alternative ways of expressing
dislike for the food. For instance, we discourage
'That's yucky. I hate it.'

3   My big rule is no toys at the table. My babysitter
reads to the kids at the table, though, so that has
kind of ruined them. They think eating is something you do when an adult entertains you

Time for an attitude adjustment.

If the French pick their battles with their children, they
fight for their mealtimes tooth and nail. When I snooped
around during mealtimes at a few French households, I
discovered that this trend of lawlessness in the *salle à
manger* has not infiltrated their ranks in the same way. In
fact, if I hadn't seen it with my own eyes, I wouldn't have
believed that a three-year-old could make a vinaigrette or
that any child under the age of seven could sit quietly,
charmingly even, all through three courses. For the most
part, French children are expected to be ready and willing to participate in family meals, including exhibiting
civil mealtime behaviour. In the same way I expect my
children to take a bath if they've rolled around in the
mud or otherwise got dirty, so the French demand that
their children eat well – in every sense. An American
acquaintance, Tilly, recounted to me her experience
dining out with her own French friend and their collective kids. Incredulous, Tilly recalled with horror her three
children climbing under the table, in the aisles, and all
over her, while the French children were seated peacefully
and calmly as they ordered, waited for, and consumed

their meals. When asked how she accomplished this, the French mother responded, 'It is non-negotiable. We pick our battles and food has a very high priority.'

The only meal in France that is approached lightly is breakfast. *Le petit dejeuner* is different from other French meals because there's only one course, but it is still no laughing matter and it is rarely consumed while multi-tasking. My kids often ask me if they can take their cereal to their rooms so that they don't have to interrupt the fascinating goings-on of their Polly Pockets or My Little Ponies. This question would not even occur to a French child, as he/she has been taught from an early age that absolutely the only place that she/he will be fed is at a table. In fact, in France they have even banned all drink and snack vending machines in the schools because of the nasty habits they breed. I've heard that if you happen to be driving on the motorway at about 1 p.m. in France, you will see cars pull over so their inhabitants can set up a little lunchtime picnic. I haven't seen this, but I do know that it is rare in France to see anyone driving around with one hand on their steering wheel and the other holding a sandwich or bap. Worse than eating on the move, however, is feasting, or even just lightly noshing, in front of a television. In both the USA and the UK, many of us parents use the television as a lure to keep our kids still and quiet so we can get some sustenance in them. Talk about bad habits! This is a major *non, non*. Recent studies have revealed that kids take in about 40 per cent more calories when they dine in front of the box. Compared with the French, it seems as though we are just fulfilling a mindless task. A potent respect for food will boost healthier mealtime practices all around. Although here in the States we can't just flip a switch and ameliorate the lunchtime spreads in our schools, being aware of the possibilities and improving the practices at our own dinner tables is a fantastic first step.

I've discovered the obvious: one way to help ensure your child will sit and eat at the dinner table is to curtail after-school snacking. I'm embarrassed to admit how often in one afternoon I cave in to pleads for a snack, but in France kids are generally allowed one snack after school, called a *goûter*, to keep them fuelled until dinner. Mind you, French parents work long hours too, and so in order to have sufficient time to put together a respectable meal, dinnertime is often much later for French kids. Perhaps my kids' *leetle* bellies will have to adjust to the sensation of not being perfectly satiated at all times. It might not be easy, but it can be done.

Although I'd seen Lucie's children behave miraculously and heard from a number of other French parents that this is not uncommon in their dining rooms, I still yearned for more proof (and tips!). I decided to spend the afternoon with Diane, another French mom I know.

We met up at about 1 p.m. and headed out to do the grocery shopping before her children arrived home from school. Immediately, there was a difference in our approaches. For me, grocery shopping means going only to the supermarket. However, for Diane, the supermarket was just the first of three stops. I was confused when she grabbed a hand basket instead of a trolley. I couldn't remember the last time I went to the supermarket and was able to fit everything into a basket. But, Diane knew what she wanted. *Tip Number 1 – know what you want when buying groceries!* 'I see so many people in American supermarkets just walking around looking and piling their shopping trolleys so high – as if they want to try everything at least once. If I know what I want and I know how to cook with it, I don't buy many unnecessary things,' she said. Together we bypassed the produce, juices, meats and deli counter – we whizzed by so many aisles that I began to wonder why we were even there at all.

Diane bought three cans of black beans, a bag of cornmeal ('I need this for a nice fish dish, and I am almost out,' she explained), butter, milk and soya milk, frozen spinach, dried lasagne noodles, a tub of yogurt and two boxes of cereal. No time was wasted in contemplation. Not a single frozen nugget was purchased. In fact, I realized that Diane had not bought one snack. When I questioned her about this she told me that her children have a couple of pieces of bread with jam after school, 'and fruit, of course'.

In Diane's estimation, Americans expect feeding to be too easy. 'I go to these homes and I see the parents look into their refrigerators worrying that there is nothing there. But there are things there – just not little packages of things that they can throw at their kids. I try not to buy the things in the little packages.' Somewhat apologetically she adds, 'Only the prepared soups will I buy – and that is because they are often better than the ones I make.' Now I know that for many of us, it is not possible to meticulously follow Diane's example as our work schedules don't always permit the same flexibility, but the spirit behind her routine is what is revolutionary.

Tip Number 2 – get over convenience. Get involved with your food. After the supermarket, Diane and I stopped at a produce market for 'about four days' worth of fruits and vegetables', and then at a upmarket shop for bread. 'What can I say, we all like nice bread.' Diane's husband was scheduled to pick up the fish on his way home from work, which she tells me is very common. 'I cannot do it all.' *Tip Number 3 – involve the whole family.*

On cue, when Diane's two children (ages five and eight) came home from school, they both drifted into the kitchen and happily devoured two pieces of fantastic-looking bread slathered in blackberry jam, after which *la cuisine a été fermée* until dinner except for a bowl of fruit on the table. Unlike in my own home, these children never feigned starvation and begged for 'just a little snack'. *Tip Number 4 – stick to the rules.* Diane assured me that the only reason her children don't beg and plead for more is because they know they won't get it. 'If they eat all afternoon, I do not think they will want their dinners.'

Diane's work schedule allows her to spend Wednesdays at home, which is why I was able to join her on her rounds. Not everyone has this same luxury, but each French parent I met with stressed, in their varying levels of English, how the quality and enjoyment of mealtimes were a main concern for them – something of top priority that they are willing to fight for. Work be damned? Sometimes. It is almost as though the entire French nation would rather quit smoking en masse than endure unruly table manners or a meal heated in the microwave. OK, that's taking it a bit far, but perhaps you see my point? Diane says, 'When I come home from work, sometimes I am very tired, but we do not order a pizza or have sandwiches for dinner. It is very important to me that we cook and have appreciation for our food. This is very French.' *Tip Number 5 – revere and respect the family meal*.

Ironically, I think Diane is more zealous with her dinners than the average French citizen because she lives in the States. In France, I noticed that people were most likely to save their extended, luxurious meals for Saturdays and Sundays and eat somewhat lightly on weekday evenings – something they can do because they know their kids have had multiple, nourishing courses at lunchtime. One French mom told me that at least once every two weeks she serves *Œuf à la coque avec des mouillettes*, which is basically just a boiled egg in a lovely egg cup with strips of toast (little soldiers – *mouillettes*) to be moistened by the yoke. Who knew that a soft-boiled egg could sound so charming.

In any event, let's push the envelope. Imagine that your kids are hungry, interested and gathered around the dinner table, which is sporting a real tablecloth, correctly set with appropriate cutlery and glasses. Go ahead, even imagine *cloth* napkins. At this point, it can't hurt to throw out a few tenets of proper French table manners:

Nombre un: Teach your children to wait until Mom places her napkin on her lap before they begin.

Nombre deux: Do not eat or drink until the mother or father says a brief blessing or toast. At my house, this requires that I actually sit down to eat with my children. That part now happens, but we've dispensed with the blessing.

Nombre trois: Apparently, it's very important that hands are kept on the table at all times. This means, *les petites mains* should never be in the lap, hanging down, or holding a Gameboy.

Nombre quatre: Bread should be placed right on the tablecloth, and not on the plate. I'm not so worried about this one.

Nombre cinq: Declining a dish is not allowed. In fact, it is a major offence. (Note: this has taken some serious work.)

Nombre six: Instruct your kids that the proper indication that they have finished eating is the placement of knife and fork together, pointing up in the centre of the plate. A wee bit uptight, perhaps?

Nombre Sept: Under no circumstance can children just leave the table without requesting to be excused *in French* (just kidding, but that would be cute). Apparently, there are some meals in France that go on for hours and hours. During these marathon meals, children are customarily allowed to leave the table and play in between courses.

Even with all of Lucie's and Diane's excellent information and tips, I was still a little worried about implementing changes in my own home. OK, utterly daunted doesn't quite convey how I was feeling about the task of recasting the shape of our meals. Bad habits, like the Terminator, die hard, and initially I couldn't really imagine anyone in my family with the willpower to 'get French' with our food, especially dinners. My husband and I are *so tired* by the end of the day, and our kids *really love* chicken nuggets and noodles slathered in spaghetti sauce from a jar – enough to want them for dinner multiple nights per week. But every time I thought about the love of food, real food, and manners (oh, the manners) demonstrated by Lucie's children, my resolve strengthened.

I'll admit it wasn't painless, by any stretch. Oona and Daphne resisted nearly every enforced modification to our previous, half-baked dinnertime practices, starting with the reduction in snacks. This shift was a particular affront, especially to Daphne, who often transformed herself into that mini John McEnroe, sprawled out with fists pounding the floor, at the outright injustice she felt when I denied her the 5 p.m. pretzels, dried mango, puffed rice snacks, and more that she'd grown accustomed to ever since sprouting teeth. In fact, even after months of practice she still grumbles about not getting sufficient junky treats, but thankfully, and perhaps because she has learned it will get her nowhere, this seems to be only on principle.

I'll gladly endure the griping, too, if that is the only trade-off for the increased appetites that come running to the table each night. And they do!

This table, by the way, has been revolutionized as well. We have made it a priority to eat, *almost* every night, all together in the dining room. Showing up for this family meal has been a piece of cake compared to the effort of feeding our kids the same meal that my husband and I consume. Before the big change, we were as unimaginative with our own dinners as we had been with the girls' food. However, knowing that the girls would certainly never agree to our nightly fare of mixed greens with some sort of meat and stinky cheese, we were forced to start planning out our dinners. If the thorn in Daphne's side is no more continuous noshing, for me it's the new pressure of thinking up a menu that is acceptable to both generations and getting the provisions to make it happen. Funny – I remember my mother complaining about this same dilemma when I was little. I am happy to report that, with practice, it gets easier every day. With a little trial and error, we are coming up with an impressive repertoire. OK, nothing remarkable (yet) by French standards, but if, six months ago, someone had told me that Oona, my finicky little kid, liked fish tacos, I never would have believed it. I have discovered that both the formality of eating in the dining room and the sense of prestige my children enjoy when they are served 'grown-up' dinners has precipitated more adventurous eating, even a heightened general interest in food. There are still plenty of nights when one or both of my girls soundly reject what they have been served, but this is surprisingly less frequent than I would have expected.

The girls have also been slow to fully embrace table manners. Recently, Oona was allowed to bring home the newly hatched chicks from her kindergarten class for the weekend. She was so excited about the visitors that her appetite evaporated, and she continually slipped away from the dinner table without permission to check on them. When I reprimanded her for bucking the new dinnertime rules, she retaliated, 'It doesn't matter, Mom! We! Are! Not! French!' (*New Tip Number 5 – Don't insert too much transparency into your endeavours.*) But despite such setbacks, we've made some very impressive strides forward.

Now that I'm on to them, I love watching little French kids relating to their food, and this is where I find the most inspiration for picking up our fondness for food at home. Clearly, the little Frenchies are bred to care about their meals. In fact, a lack of culinary appreciation can even be used as an insult for kids. I was watching the movie *Les enfants de Timpelbach* on a plane once and laughed bits of omelette au fromage out of my nose when one of the film's enfants insulted another with the line, 'Ta mère est une vegetarianne!' I've got nothing against vegetarians, but that putdown was impossible to resist. Is a non-foie-gras-eating mother the French equivalent to our 'Your Mama is so fat' jokes?

With my new bright attitude, I realize that I have got a

lot more than determination on my side. I'm not sure if Michelle Obama had the time-worn French routines in mind when she decided to keep fresh fruit out for her own girls to cut down on other, less wholesome snacks, or if Jamie Oliver visited any Parisian school lunch rooms before he set out on *Jamie Oliver's Food Revolution*, his 2010 television show which aimed to improve the sorry state of our dietary habits in the States (often zeroing in on our school cafeterias), but something good is clearly going on. Farmers markets are popping up across the States like bubbles in a nearly completed beurre blanc sauce, there's a movement here to ban fizzy drinks in school vending machines, 'locavore' is almost a common-place word, and even Wal-Mart is pushing organic produce. *Vive la Révolution*!

6

Les Plaisirs Simples or
The Gift of Less

If you were at all alarmed by the difference in accumulation tendencies between expectant French and American and British couples discussed earlier, I'm afraid to report that these inclinations don't stop when the baby is born. What with all the bribing, celebrations and general sense of entitlement bred in our kids – they tend to amass way too much. And the worst part is that they end up playing with about 2 per cent of it – give or take the odd, forgotten Polly Pocket.

They don't have the same problem in France. This is due to the boundaries and discipline the French are so damn good at instilling. Yet just because one is aware of *how* something is done, doesn't mean one can do it. I understand the basic physics of how a plane flies, but there ain't no way I am pilot material.

This is to say that, with two kids who thought it was an innate human right to have their every material desire fulfilled, I needed real tips on elegantly (or not) denying them these desires. When Oona and Daphne were tiny, it was relatively easy to keep their little hearts singing with cheap trinkets from bubblegum machines and tatty knick-knacks. But then they graduated to slightly classier, and more expensive, obsessions. But still I would say to myself, 'What's $13 for a stuffed otter when it makes her *sooo* happy?'

Well, that love of an otter has now morphed into the painful *need* of a Nintendo DS. All of a sudden, poor Oona is now hearing from us, 'If you want something, you have to earn it.' Not long ago I actually heard myself say, 'Money doesn't grow on trees.' Out loud. It's no wonder that this isn't sitting very well with Oona – she has never really been introduced to the concept of financial responsibility. It is not because we have tons of money to toss about, we just didn't want to disappoint. For instance, when the holidays would roll around, every time my kids mentioned a dream toy, I would secretly put it in my Amazon shopping cart, telling myself I'd edit the list later. But I rarely did. For the past six years, this is how the negotiations generally went:

Me: Mac, I have to buy the girls' presents. Come look at my Amazon list and help me decide.

Mac: Oh, great work, babe. They will love this stuff. I say just get everything. You know my theory – if we can possibly afford it, we should give them the best Christmas and Chanukah possible. Also, you don't need to get me anything.

Me: Totally. And don't get me anything either.

Here I go.

Proceed to Checkout

So not only would the kids end up with way too much loot, but Mac and I gave one another nothing – a really bad way to keep the home fires burning, if you know what I mean. Up until now, the kids have never asked for anything extravagant (except for the traditional request for a pony, but I was easily able to explain that Santa does not roll with livestock). After speaking with French parents, I realized that our approach, although motivated by love and a wish to see our kids go gaga with glee on Christmas morning, has been irresponsible. On my last trip to France I struck up a conversation with a French couple on the TGV (fastest train in the world!), parents of eight-year-old twin girls who were on their way to meet their children at a grandparent's house in the countryside, and I ended up describing a typical Christmas morning in our house. They were a bit scandalized. 'Oh, I don't know . . .' said the French dad, 'You should not get them so much, I think. No. Maybe you are not helping them this way. You are just making people that want everything. This will not be so fun for anyone.' The French certainly are opinionated – but often spot on when it comes to this sort of thing.

What about Chanukah? Well, my husband's family is Jewish on his mother's side. However, it was mostly his grandmother who kept the Jewish culture alive (and still does with the Chanukah cheques, alarmingly delicious brisket, and genius gallows humour). In the thick of his childhood, Mac's parents were both practising Sufis, regularly zipping off to meetings and meditation sessions with fellow followers of the Eastern philosophy. His dad was raised Protestant and his mom's family, while Jewish, were practising atheists. That's all to say that he celebrated both Christmas and Chanukah – and, similarly, with our kids we decided to throw it all in there. Double Happiness! Fun! Eight days of Chanukah booty in addition to Christmas has to ensure great childhood memories, our thinking went. I can now tell you what it does ensure – a stockpile of plastic crap in every corner of the house.

I laughed when Oona came home from school one year ecstatic because she'd learned that Yom Kippur was coming up. 'Mommy! I'm part Jewish so I am supposed to celebrate. What do we get?' She dropped the subject when I told her she was entitled to fast for twenty-five hours.

I remember exactly when my feelings of squeamishness about all this curdled into something much more rotten. In a conversation with Juliette, a French mother from Normandy, I asked, 'How often do your kids receive presents?' She thought for a moment and responded, 'Three times a year. They will get a present on their birthday, one on the last day of school – that's a little something I do because they have worked so hard all of the year – and then on Chanukah.' Juliette was raised Catholic, but her American husband is Jewish so she converted, and they've chosen a side when it comes to the full-on holidays. Full-on here in the States, anyway. My husband and I aren't religious – but we do like the lively traditions. Still hoping that I wouldn't feel like a complete glutton, I asked Juliette to describe the types of presents she gives. 'On the birthdays they get one nice thing, usually. My son wanted that video game you can hold in your hands, so that is what we got him.'

'Um, anything else?' – I had to ask.

'Well, yes,' Juliette said.

Aha!

'His father's family sent a big box of things from the States.'

Deep sigh.

Juliette's end-of-school-year *blowout* present sounds like something I would get my kids if they'd been tolerable at the end of a really long drive – a game or stuffed animal.

What really got me, though, was what she'd given her son for Chanukah the previous year. 'He was crazy for this big, expensive Star Wars Lego set. So, we bought him the set. I separated the pieces into seven little bags, and we gave him one bag each night. Then, on the last night we gave him the instructions so he could put it all together. He was so happy.'

If I gave my kids partial presents, they would tie me up and poke me with the Pick-up-Stix that Oona demanded on our last trip to the shopping mall. Oona's and Daphne's expectations are way too high for that kind of parcelling, and I'm not sure we will ever get there. But Juliette did make me reconsider the routine frenzy that went on in our house on Christmas morning and, when the paroxysm was over, the kind of letdown that always occurred until, inevitably, one of my kids sheepishly mentioned something they were hoping for but didn't get. You kidding me?

That's the part I always blocked out. It was time for some unpleasant, honest introspection. Real talk, as it were. I saw our overindulgence as vulgar and not the values that I wanted to be passing down to my kids. There is a way to have great memories without guaranteeing the need of a new landfill every 25 December. A little French bird (OK, French dad) mentioned that they like to set limits on the gift giving. So, for the holidays last year my husband and I made an agreement – we shook on it! – that we would buy the girls three things each for Christmas (not including the Christmas stockings, but I went old-school on those – sweets, toothbrushes and socks). We did the Chanukah candles every night as well, and Oona and Daphne each received only one small prize on the eighth night. *C'est fini.*

The reduction of material offerings did nothing to reduce everyone's enjoyment. It may sound illogical, but Oona and Daphne actually seemed happier with what they received *and* there was no discernible anticlimax. Who knew?

Not all French families are as restrained as Juliette – who is financially very well off, by the way – when it comes to doling out the goods. Even so, most other *familles Française* don't even begin to approach the kind of material blitzkrieg that takes place in a typical

American or British household during the holidays. When it comes to Christmas, the French tend to concentrate on the food just as keenly as the gifts (that makes perfect sense for a country that spends more time eating than any other), and in many households the gifts are not exchanged until Christmas evening (again, not surprising as people in France also spend more time sleeping than people in any other country). I can still easily make myself merry in June if I think about Christmas morning, so I'm not about to mess with our schedule; I am just going to try to modulate the windfall a bit. When I'm feeling weak, I love to conjure up Juliette and her treatment of the Star Wars Lego set. Last year, my nephew's Christmas list had ninety-two items on it. If he played with each of them during his waking hours on Christmas Day, that would leave about ten minutes per present. I get dizzy just thinking about such a whiplash playing pace. Oh, and I'm not saying that it is French-style for multi-culti families to pick a team and ignore one side of the family's heritage – I'm just advocating for some self-control all around. We are so intensely focused on guaranteeing that our kids' dreams come true – even if those dreams involve bottling unicorn breath from an island made of rainbows – that we tend to lose our minds. I want my kids to remember the magic of affection and tradition around the holidays, and not just the piles of plunder. And this year, I think I'll redirect some of those funds and get something nice for my husband.

Certainly of note, by the way, is Pre Fouettard, French Santa's manager-like sidekick. A bit of a disciplinarian really, this character flies around with Père Noël on Christmas Eve, gleefully reminding him of the children that do not deserve presents because of some shoddy behaviour. He sounds like a total prat, but I kind of wish we had one here.

Of course, if I am going to redesign Santa's parameters, I'm also going to need to renovate our Easter tradition as well. Instead of the resurrection of Christ, Easter has somehow become more like the rebirth of Christmas for my kids. Last year, their enormous Easter baskets still weren't roomy enough for the mountain of toys and sweets I tried to cram in. Then, I had to go and ask a French friend, Marc, about Easter in his country: 'The kids have the eggs and nice chocolate, and there are baskets, but it is not so extreme as I've seen for you in the USA. Actually, nowhere in the world is as extreme as for you. Oh, except for the Philippines at Christmastime.' Alright, take it easy, Marc. And also, I'm not sure I'll go with the flying bells that French kids are told bring on the goods (makes about as much sense as the Easter Bunny), but I am certain that Monsieur Cottontail is going to chill out on the spoils a bit. From what I gather, the French focus almost strictly on fine chocolates for the kids. This I can do.

Then there's Valentine's Day – another tradition of growing immoderation brought to American and British kids by corporations. I am going to have to stay strong – and French-ish.

If you are tempted to pity Oona and Daphne here, don't. They've been at sea in an ocean of extravagance for too long. I knew we had hit a wall when we experienced what is now known as 'Lunchbox Waterloo'. One day in kindergarten, a little decorative flower fell off Daphne's beloved Hello Kitty lunchbox. Because the girls get new lunchboxes every year, I assured her that she had a few backups for the choosing. I'd forgotten, however, that one lunchbox (super cute with pink polka dots) had been committed to hold our parakeet Marvin Montandon's birdseed. When I offered two choices to the kid for replacing Hello Kitty, you would have thought I was suggesting that she carry her lunch to school in a bedpan. 'But, but, but – that's not fair! I want to have three more! That's what I *need*.' At the risk of sounding all, 'I walked six miles uphill to school in the snow in my day', I used a brown bag when I was a kid – not a trendy, mega-expensive, hand-stitched, monogrammed satchel, or a customized 'modular lunchbox system', or even, God forbid, something metal, covered with lead paint with a matching thermos flask.

Now, mercifully, we are deep into detritus detox, scaling back and talking *a lot* about excess. The French don't worry too much about lunchboxes, what with those four-course meals served at school, but when I looked into their approach to backpacks, I found that the same backpack can last a long time. You also don't see many television characters and cartoons adorning their gear. If Daphne were French, she'd have to be sporting La Petite Mermaid on her back for the next four years.

I received a surprise lesson in teaching the value of money from a French pal, Christiane, who lives on the

Upper East Side of Manhattan. I happened to be over one day when her parents were visiting from Lyon. Both Christiane and her mother were engaged in a very serious conversation with Christiane's eight-year-old daughter, Marie, who was desperate for an American Girl doll. Marie looked stricken – and I could tell that her dreams of acquiring a Kit Kittredge or a Julie Albright were being dashed, but after a long, hushed conversation, she wiped her eyes and gave both her mother and grandmother a kiss. Later, I pressed Christiane for details. What was the problem? 'Well, quite frankly, that is just too much money for a doll. My mother would like to get her a present, and she doesn't mind spending money – but how will Marie ever understand the value of money if we are spending $120 on one doll. It is really too much. This is not easy to explain to a child, but it is necessary. It was a big deal for her, but it's also an important idea for her to understand.' Cringe moment no. 927 for me. When my *four-year-old* asked for an American Girl doll, I merely passed along the wish to her grandfather, who happily complied as he was desperate for a birthday present idea. (Note: this is my husband's father, who I believe owns one pair of trousers and saves on his water bill by not showering. Daddy Warbucks he most certainly is not – but no one Stateside is immune from fiscal fever, particularly when there are kids involved.) It didn't even occur to me that this was inappropriate or could be a learning opportunity for my children. Oona ended up getting one of these very dear – and, yes, very well made – dolls as well. The French are all about teaching the respect of money to their children, and in private because money is unmentionable in polite society. I felt like a bit of a boob after watching the care and responsibility Christiane brought to the subject. A few months later, however, my boob-o-meter flew way off the charts. That's when Daphne took her Julie doll to a friend's house, covered it with make-up, and gave it a haircut. I felt more negligent and profligate than ever.

Christiane's example has really stuck with me. I no longer just hand out change from our little glass jar in the kitchen every time my children ask for money, which happens often when they are deep in a fantasy game of 'grocery store' or 'library' (Oona, ever the creative entre-preneur, likes to make her dolls pay fines). Daphne has no idea what a dime is worth, and I'm not even sure what she did when she finished playing with the coins I so casually dolled out. We now talk about the responsibility that comes with money. It seems so obvious and import-ant to me now, but this is the kind of thing that gets overlooked in our current childrearing climate of 'make them happy at any cost'. Believe me, Christiane did not enjoy declining Marie's request, but she did it in an attempt to create a thoughtful, conscientious person. Funny part is, the mother of one of Marie's wealthy schoolmates ended up giving Marie her first American Girl doll – figuring that the poor kid wanted it so much and needed it, really, for the girls to play together.

The first time Oona asked for an allowance she was three years old. I'm not even sure she knew what the word meant – except that it was something she should have, which would allow her to get more of the things that she wanted. She must have heard about it at daycare or in an episode of *Scooby-Doo!* This, of course, was well before we attempted to get French – so Mac and I thought the request was precocious and cute (made even cuter because she used to talk with a little lisp), and we ceremoniously gave her 15 cents from that kitchen change jar every Friday, which she would dutifully transfer to her Hello Kitty bank. As she, and now Daphne, grow older, we've tried to make them earn the ever-growing sum. (At around age five, Oona caught on that 15 cents wasn't getting her anywhere and most recently asked for $5 a week. For doing nothing. At least I had the sense to deny that one.) Regrettably, neither of my girls is tremendously fond of chores. And yet, they thought a weekly handout was a privilege that naturally came along with being a kid. Sorry, lovies – not so in France! I found that few young French children are given any allowance at all. The value of money is such that small kids needn't be trusted with it. And because they don't have the same fixation on stuff in a consumer culture, they don't yearn for it. But of course they are still expected to do chores. I did speak with one set of French parents who dole out the cash – but on a 'per job' basis. In addition to the regular, obligatory household duties, their kids can complete other chores to earn money. For instance, organizing the Tupperware brings in half a Euro. On our snazzy new 'jobs board', I've agreed to a quarter for dusting the living room, 15 cents for sorting laundry, and 20 cents for (effectively) wiping down the triptych of tables including the ones in the kitchen, dining and living rooms. Everyone wins! At first Oona was a little too enthusiastic – she's hell bent on getting an iPod Shuffle and has accepted that we aren't just going to buy it willy-nilly – and I began to fear for the bank account, so we've limited the extras to no more than six bonus jobs a week. Still, my house is much more tidy these days.

There remains a lot to be learned about excess. With two kids in the bloom of their birthday party careers, I have thrown (and attended) some real doozies. I've always felt particularly lucky that my girls were born in the 'good weather' months, so that we could host their birthday parties in the park. I truly feel bad for those parents saddled with a February birthday to exalt their offspring. Here in New York City, parents regularly shell out upwards of $500 for a party. What else can they do? That's what everyone else does. And apparently, it's not just the weather that's to blame. A friend from Los Angeles recently confided in me that he's in the market to buy a bouncy castle: 'At nine out of ten – no, maybe ten out of ten – birthday parties here there is a bouncy castle. If we get one, we'll save a ton on the rental.' Even by throwing Oona and Daphne parties in the park, I was never able to keep costs under $250. There's the requisite pizza for thirty people, drinks, snacks for parents, cake, piñata, balloons for everyone, and goodie bags. *Goodie bags* – the bane of birthday parties. There is nothing less cute than a little guest at a party screeching, 'Where are the goodie bags? What do we get?' With mortification, I will admit that it has once been mine (but not since she got an earful about that). Inevitably, there is crying and disappointment because some kid got the wrong colour trinket in their bag of favours, or they only like chocolate but received Gummi Bears. Also, goodie bags are *always* filled with plastic junk that I immediately throw away. The whole thing is a wasteful hassle, really.

These kinds of birthday bonanzas are not standard in France. I attended *l'anniversaire* of a French five-year-old while I was abroad. It was a revelation. He had two friends over to share his favourite meal of roasted chicken and potato wedges and chocolate cake (all expertly cooked by his parents, naturally). It was so simple and refreshing – and strangely more enjoyable for everyone than any kid's party I can remember attending in Brooklyn, where, more often than not, the birthday kid ends up having a breakdown because of all the attention and stimulation – and sugar. I am still trying to get the blood out of a shirt Oona wore to the last party we attended – a vicious game of freeze tag, don't ask – where things went so berserk that three children ended up with bloody noses. Iron Maiden would've envied the decibel level in that room. And how do the French handle goodie bags? According to a friend who teaches in an elementary school in Paris and has two daughters, 'There are none of these at French birthday parties. The child should not be rewarded for going to a party. He gets to go and have fun and eat cake. That is surely enough.' Once more with feeling: *touché*. Many of the French acknowledged having more of a 'thing' when their babies turned one – a real milestone – but beyond that there's often just a family party until the kids get a little older and are allowed a couple of friends to celebrate with them.

Again with the detox, we have decided that Oona and Daphne are going to take a year off parties, starting this year. True, we're still a few months away from either of their birthdays and this is all a bit theoretical, but so far they seem strangely accepting of the arrangement. Also, as I am trying to be at least part French, they don't have a whole lot of say on the matter. They will be given a birthday party every *other* year. This is hardly a bad deal for them. On the off-year, they get to be 'Queen for a Day', which entails choosing what's for breakfast (we used to do that anyway, but I think they may have forgotten), going to a toy store and selecting whatever they want (within price-tag reason), and deciding where we go to dinner. If I could get them to be excited about home-roasted chicken, I'd make it every night, but they haven't become *that* French yet. Alas, for now we are still at the mercy of a diner or pizza parlour. I have explained that their future birthdays will not yield a pile of presents, carted home in a rubbish bag post-party. So far they don't seem bothered by this. Is it possible that, in some small way, they are relieved? I know I am.

I realized that something had to give (and suspected that the French had the answer) when I grew fanatical about jettisoning playthings from my home. Every time my kids left the house and I was left in glorious solitude, I would fiendishly dart to their bedroom with a rubbish bag and start filling it up with toys. This will sound pathetic to any non-parents out there, but this was almost more fun for me than going to see a film or going out for a drink. The first couple of times I was tentative – 'This glow-in-the-dark turtle is so nice. They might want to play with it *some* day.' So, I'd fill a rubbish bag and put it in the cupboard for a few months to gauge the sturdiness of my resolve. I've done this on three different occasions, and not once have they noticed anything missing. They'd commented that their room seemed 'cleaner' and 'bigger', but they hadn't been able to pinpoint what was not there any more. Guess they weren't very attached. So now I've removed the 'holding bay' cupboard stage, and the hapless junk goes straight to the secondhand shop as fast as I can get it there. To my delight, I've discovered that my kids are actually playing with the remaining toys more now. It's as though the survivors look more desirable now that the plastic overgrowth has been hacked away and they can actually be seen. When the girls' room was bursting at the seams, they'd walk in and complain, 'There's nothing to play with!' But now, with less to play with, I rarely hear the lament. I have a friend who swears that the same logic works with clothing. She's always giving me cast-off clothes, which she claims get in the way when she's trying to put together outfits. I should probably stop taking them – since I rarely end up wearing them. But *some* day I might.

The French seem very keyed into this little trick. I've been watching a lot of French films lately, and I'm always freshly shocked at the depiction of children's spaces. I cannot think of one French film that has a kid's room brimming with stuff (I thought I'd found a culprit in the

film *Noémie: le secret* until I realized it is Canadian.)
This is certainly not the case with many American films,
classics even, from *E.T.* to *Toy Story*. Art imitating life? I
am sure the incredible, expanding nursery exists here and
there in French cinema, but it is certainly not the norm.
It's also not the norm in true French homes, as a little bit
of sleuthing on my part revealed. 'Discreet' is the word
that comes to mind when I think about the existence of
toys in the French homes I visited. And these were homes
that often housed more children than the average family
of four in my circles. As the French government truly
rewards its citizens for procreating, the third (and fourth!)
child is far from rare. Yet, somehow their homes, even the
children's rooms, don't morph into enormous playrooms,
as is the trend in the States. My heart melted during a
tour of a little six-year-old French girl's room. Her
English was even worse than my French, so it wasn't so
much what she said, but rather the way she handled her
moderate amount of belongings with such affection. She
had two baby dolls (not nine, which is the last tally from
my girls' room – not including the now contentious
American Girl dolls). Get ready to be inspired – and a tad
jealous. If French children can play happily and independently with fewer things, so can ours. Easing off on the
attention and the constant cascade of presents appears to
do wonders for the imagination of a child.

I've seen it work with the toys, and I'm determined to
practise the same kind of regulation in my wardrobe.
Gone are the days of carefree amassing. It's time for some
serious weeding and tough decisions. My French lady

friends tell me it is all about concentrating on a few qual-ity, pivotal pieces that look great and will last. Maybe that explains the 'classic' French look.

It's time to talk about damn prizes. Like most of the kids in our neighbourhood, somehow my daughters had begun to expect a prize for everything, from getting a haircut to accompanying me to fill the car up with petrol.

I know that there are certain situations that I cannot and, to be honest, don't really want to get out of with-out giving my kids something special. For example, Daphne is completely petrified of the doctor. We've had enough conversations about her well-being and the necessity of check-ups that she's accepted the fact that she has to go – but she still doesn't like it. At all. She and I struck a deal that, whenever she gets an injection, I will buy her a prize. It's always a harrowing experience (a couple of times, because of some very impressive writhing and theatrics, we've even had to abort the mission and reschedule), but when she does get through it, I'm usually so relieved that it's over, and heartbroken for poor, tortured, hoarse-from-screaming Daphne, that we head straight to the nearest toy store and am there relieved once again – this time of at least $35 for a pity prize. I know a French five-year-old, Christian, with the same kind of doctor phobia, and I asked his father how they deal with the situation: 'We are like you, and we always allow Christian a little *cadeau* after the doctor ordeal. He had his flu injection last time, so after it was over I took him to the stationery store and I bought him two rolls of tape.' Tape! How brilliant. And

I'm sure Daphne would have much more fun with a few spoils from the stationery store (she has a real thing for Post-It notes) than the 150th stuffed animal that she inevitably picks out. And even a jumbo stack of multi-coloured Post-It notes probably cost less than a cup of coffee. *Voila* – another problem solved.

The truth is, my children are far more enjoyable now that I've put a stop to the bribes and exchange of perks for good conduct. Ever since the font went mostly dry (read: French) they don't expect it. Occasionally, the spirit will move me and I will get them something unexpected and they are *sooo* happy. Much happier than they used to be when the goods rained down. Our new favourite thing to do with the girls is to go out for dinner. They're suddenly capable of remaining seated at a table in public, waiting for their food, eating with utensils and decorum, and hanging around with my husband and me until everyone is ready to go. My heart sank a bit when I read about a new restaurant nearby that features video screens in the table tops, so that parents can enjoy a dinner out in a restaurant while their kids watch movies. To me, this is beyond depressing. I've seen so many French children, as young as two, sit through long luxurious meals without the need of a screen to keep them from exploding, crawling under the table, or throwing silverware. I'm no flower-child and my kids know all of their Disney characters off pat, but I think there's something sad about having to plug them in for a family meal – especially at a restaurant.

I've been truly inspired by French children and their

lack of dependence on *la télévision*. It is difficult to provide exact statistics of the television consumption of French and American and British kids as there are countless studies and the numbers appear to change daily (not for the better, I'm afraid), but it's safe to say that French children spend less time staring slack-jawed at the box. It seems as if every day there is another news article about the detrimental effects of television time on young, developing brains. In 2008 the French television authority banned channels from programming any shows directed at children under three years old – while this is a booming market here in the States. A probable reason for the difference in older French kids is that network French television is reputedly ghastly so the temptation isn't the same, as well as the fact that it's not as easy in France to get 600 channels beamed in to your home. Regardless of the grounds for the disparity, I'm convinced that those little French kids receive a boost in their powers of self-amusement because they have more time in the day to practise. In France little kids don't count on coming home from school and cuddling up with Dora or Phineas and Ferb (the big ones have too much homework to do). I had always thought of television as having a calming effect, but a little light bulb went off during one auspicious multicultural, multigenerational party. Three families had gathered for lunch at the loft apartment of a mutual good friend. Oona, Daphne and two young Frenchies represented the kids' contingent. I had brought along the portable DVD player, figuring that at some point we could throw on a DVD to ensure a little adult peace. After playing blissfully with the French kids for over an hour, Daphne, while looking for some fairy gear in my bag (I usually travel with at least one wand and a tiara), realized what I'd got and begged me to put on a DVD. The other kids joined in, and soon they were all deep into an Angelina Ballerina DVD. We parents had been so thrilled that the kids were playing so well that we specified only one episode. After thirty minutes of watching Angelina's antics in a tutu, the four children returned to their game. Unfortunately, they had a really hard time finding their groove again, and they clashed more than anything else. I usually like to blame these mood swings on fatigue or hunger, but they'd all eaten well and it was only 2 p.m. Then, the French mother dropped a giant revelation on me: 'It is the television. They always fight when they watch television. It takes a while for them to use their own brains again after watching.' While I'd always told my children that television rots the brain and other savoury axioms that come gratis with the parenting handbook, I'd never really seen it in practice. Or, at least I hadn't put it together. Ever since we've cut back on the television time at home, sibling battles have most definitely waned.

To determine exactly how to cut back, I turned to the French. No doubt, there isn't just one way to do things in France, and the answers I got on how much television is enough are all over the map. A few separate sources said that they only allow their kids to watch videos that 'have a beginning and an end. A real story, and not just cartoons or sitcoms – I also read once that the Obamas have a similar rule in their house (OK, the White House) and they all sure seem smart!' This seems like good advice, but a little too stringent for me. I happen to love mindless cartoons. My new French-*inspired* approach is to only allow screen time (including computer and iPad) at the weekends. Although counter-intuitive, this rule has made our lives much easier. Oona and Daphne don't even bother begging for it on weekday mornings or when they get home from school any more. Before the rule was in place, I spent valuable energy negotiating television time. My kids were either livid or insufferable whine-bags if I dared to reject a morning show. It was often just easier to let them have their way and feed and dress them in front of the box. These days, our mornings are often lovely, with a shared breakfast and more time for dressing and playing (and maybe a little leftover homework).

There was also the happy realization that we are sending the message that dinner together is more important than television in the evenings. Very French, indeed. I had a good laugh on a recent Tuesday night when, while we were sitting around the table, my husband mistakenly announced, 'After you clear the table, I'm going to show you guys a really funny YouTube video.' As the new heavy in the house, it was my duty to point out that the kids aren't allowed to watch videos on weekday evenings. The sadness in the dining room at that moment was palpable, so I gave in: 'OK, you can watch Daddy's YouTube clip, but only tonight. This is highly irregular so don't get used to it.' The video itself, starring a kitten on a trampoline, was under three minutes, but before it was cued up,

Oona and Daphne spent close to fifteen minutes dancing and hugging and laughing. They were *beyond* giddy that I was going to let them watch something. Anything. For a moment, after I stopped giggling at the spectacle, I wondered if I was being cruel in our routine of not allowing television when it made them this happy. But that's the thing – it had never made them this happy. Now that screen time is truly special and my kids don't consider it a right, it has taken on a whole new meaning for them.

I know that cutting out television completely during the week is not feasible for many families (here and in France), yet I think we can take a cue from French parents and create a few (almost) unbendable rules to decrease television's dominion in the home. Or, if you've got the uber cable situation, you could try only allowing programming in French – I'm sure that would crush some of the appeal.

What does all this mean for school holidays? I was tempted to consider most of summertime and any non-school day in the same camp as 'weekend'. I've made such a big deal about television interfering with their focus on school that I didn't really have a leg to stand on in, say, late August, with no camp or school in sight. Once again, I suffered that now very familiar feeling that I was rather half-hearted in my Frenchification efforts when I was setting up interviews with French families, and a large number of them apologetically informed me that they would be unavailable for the month of August because they would not have phone or internet connection. Paris in late summer is taken over by tourists, as the city's natives have fled to their centuries-old, rustic and perfectly romantic farmhouses (gross generalization here, but much of the population does hoof it somewhere else). Eventually, it dawned on me that a place without the phone or internet probably also doesn't have mini-golf, multiplex cinemas, video game arcades, or any of the other 'amusements' that we've been accustomed to dishing out to the kids during the holidays. What do the French do all day with their kids in such a place? Not much, as it turns out. But the twist? Apparently they love it. Marguerite, a French mother of twins, said to me: 'The children like to relax and it's very nice for them to play outside. And they like to garden with me.' It all sounded so quaint and, I must say, healthy, yet I could not – and did not – want to imagine my own kids after two days on holiday without their beloved NetFlix or Nick Jr computer games, not to mention no hope of diversions tailored specifically to their kind (the even more dreaded Chuck E. Cheese). But, what kind of French-parenting wannabe was I if I didn't at least try?

So, I created my own faux French countryside.

Experimenting on children sounds so sinister, and I don't want to get some kind of reputation as a Mommy Mengele or anything, but I'm positively elated by the results of this one.

For a number of reasons, I couldn't quite get my entire family to the real French countryside, so I did the best I could to recreate the experience much closer to home. Happily, it was not as hard to do as I thought, and we found our little getaway Française in a remarkably close yet still sufficiently secluded hamlet on Fire Island, located off the south shore of Long Island. Just a two-hour train ride to a ferry, and in another half-hour we felt very far away from Brooklyn. On our part of the island, which is 330 yards at its widest and only 190 yards at its most narrow, there is only one little market and one restaurant. Not a lot of opportunity to placate kids with consumer crap.

Still, I hadn't fully realized when we made the Fire Island arrangements just how perfect it was for our purposes. With no cars allowed on the island, I was barred from chickening out and stockpiling backup toys and other diversions for the girls. It was time to sink or swim. Oona and Daphne were each allowed to bring whatever they wanted, provided it would fit in their small backpacks, which they would be carrying themselves. (Lucie had once chastised me for always schlepping their things: 'You are a mom, not a mule.') Of course, it would not have taken much effort at all to stock the iPad with games and movies and slip it into our (one!) suitcase, but I was hell bent on getting this right, so we left all screens at home. I was more than a little nervous, to be sure. I summoned thoughts of books like *Heidi* and *Little House on the Prairie* for inspiration. When I'd stop and realize that I was worrying about how my children would respond when given only a wonderful beach house, gorgeous seashore and a nearby bay filled with clams and crabs to entertain them, I felt like a sad and privileged city idiot.

On the downside, Fire Island, rather unfortunately,

rivals New York City when it comes to things like the cost of food. To make my ersatz French getaway possible, we rented one big, beautifully ramshackle six-bedroom house with a revolving cast of good friends, including Paul, a fashion industry exec from Bordeaux who has been living in the States for the past four years. The conditions were practically perfect for my summer experiment.

Despite our near translucence, my husband and I both love the beach and the sea, so this was hardly the first sand-filled holiday that the girls had been on. Previously, however, we had stayed primarily in beach motels, all with pools and usually located in towns that twinkled in the night – not because of the stars overhead but because of gaudily packed boardwalks blinking crazily with flashing rides, games, and neon signs saluting junk food aplenty. During these other holidays, the beach turned out to be among the lowlights for the girls (down there with teeth brushing) – just a backdrop to the glitz of the ferris wheel and the curiously timeless thrill of a pink wad of candy floss the size of a well-fed bunny. Generally the kids would consent to an hour – tops – playing in the surf to appease us so we would let them go back in the pool or to the ice cream parlour. Oona often griped that the beach was 'just way too sandy'.

And so I set off for Fire Island lugging only a single suitcase – but also plenty of trepidation. I could easily envisage how ten days of isolation with minimal toys, no electronic entertainment, and copious amounts of sand could end in disaster.

But somehow it didn't. In fact, it was the most

enjoyable family holiday we have ever had. I'm not about to live off-grid or anything – I may be second only to my husband in the contest for least handy person on Earth – but I saw in a short time how my children, given no other choice, learned the art of hanging out. And oh, what a fantastically gorgeous art that is.

An alternate title to this book could be *Why French Kids can Hang: And What it Means for their Parents*. It is such a beautiful thing when a once petulant kid comes out of the whiney woods. I realized on Fire Island that I may have been inadvertently banishing my two to the forest. Maybe, in our former attempts to ensure that our kids had fun on holiday, we had, in effect, prevented them (and us) from reaching new levels of enjoyment. Really, there is only so much fun to be had on the Frog-Hopper – you go up and then . . . you go down – and the constant stimulation and seduction of the carnival atmosphere would turn my kids into holy terrors. We'd been separating their pleasure from our own – somewhat grudgingly taking them to the kids' entertainments, and then 'escaping' to do something grown-up one night with the assistance of the hotel babysitter – always uneasy about leaving our kids with a stranger and unhappy about all of the added expenses. Having seen many French children mingling, but not dominating, in the adult realm without consistent embellishments, I had a new goal for my own children.

Knowing that we didn't pack any films or video games, the girls wasted very little time begging for them. Even if they'd been particularly persuasive, there was nowhere to go and buy, or even rent, media for a Muppet Fix. Brilliant. Naturally, they fell into a rhythm of playing with each other and the grown-ups. In hindsight, it was fortuitous for my little ploy that most of my friends on the trip were childless. These pals are not accustomed to the trends of permissiveness in parenting, and thus were not inclined to indulge my children when it came to any dictatorial behaviour. With Mac and me cranking up the French amid a group of adults who wanted only to enjoy their own time off, Oona and Daphne were completely outnumbered.

My fears that they would be tiny misery machines were put to rest almost immediately, and they took to nature like burrowing sand crabs. We spent hours and hours building sandcastles, playing wave tag, going on scenic walks (walks! Ha!), reading, playing board games and baking. Ah yes, the baking. This is where Paul took over the French education of my kids, especially if they dared to announce that there was nothing to do: 'What? If you are bored then we must do some work. You know the dessert will not make itself. Now stop complaining and put on *dees* apron.' My kids are now well practised in the arts of chocolate mousse, peach tatin and, of course, crème brûlée. Oona and Daphne wanted to teach Paul a thing or two about the confectionary arts as well. After they introduced him to 's'mores' (the dubiously delicious combination of chocolate, graham crackers and marsh-mallows), he effectively damned their two favourite sweets in one fell strike, 'Well, it's not nearly as bad as that Rice Krispie treat.'

All of this successful hanging out brought to mind a recent conversation I'd had with Bess, one of my Brooklyn mom friends. She was nervous about a forthcoming holiday at her husband's parents' house (Bess's relationship with her mother-in-law is a perfect cliché). She complained, 'It's always awkward when we go there for holidays now because there are no kids running around creating buffers like there used to be. I mean, all of the little cousins are there, but everyone has their own computer or Nintendo DS, and it has become much quieter. I'm always stuck in the kitchen with just grown-ups, trying to get along.' There was so much to pity in Bess's situation, but the thought of kids spending more time with their machines than with each other at an annual party is particularly saddening.

There's no doubt that the past seven years of childrearing have given me countless marvellous memories, and many of them spring from our family trips – but these ten days on Fire Island were truly transcendent. It was the first time since having children that my husband and I felt that the holiday was not all about the kids. Very refreshingly, Oona and Daphne had to figure out a way to adapt to the adult world, and not the other way around. This is an integral concept in French parenting. Once they understood this, and that none of the grown-ups present thought it was cute or even appropriate for them to always be hogging centre stage, they adapted. In fact, I think they even realized that it was to their advantage. With a little patience and daring, they were allowed access to a new side of their parents – one that is not always catering to them. I saw them looking at us with something close to wonder. For me, this was extraordinarily moving. I want them to have these kinds of memories of me, and not just recollections of me as a parent. When they are in their thirties, they will want to know what I was like at their age. At least they will if they are anything like me, constantly trying to remember my own mother as a person separate from her identity as a mom.

I knew we were on to something when, on our second night on Fire Island, the girls asked if they could stay up and have dinner with the grown-ups. As the adults were planning to eat at 9 p.m., I felt conflicted. I agreed on the condition that they control themselves. I made it very clear that both their father and I wanted to enjoy the company of our friends, and that they would be visitors at our table and not permitted to rule it. For Daphne who was, well, Daphne and only four years old, I assumed this would be a real challenge – for all of us. But that dinner was sublime. The kids were calm and courteous, instinctively knowing that complaining about being tired or about what was put on their plates would detrimentally affect their future requests to join our adult posse. They hung around the table with us for over an hour, and when we started dancing, my girls curled up on a daybed on the screened-in porch – still unwilling to leave a gaggle of grown-ups clearly having fun. I'm not sure when they fell asleep, but it was with satisfaction and unforgettable pride that Mac and I, drunk on life and plenty of red wine, transferred our two sleeping beauties upstairs to bed.

On this trip, we pared down the excesses and turned up the trust in our kids' inherent coolness. It was a gamble that totally paid off. Our faux-French holiday has been the most gratifying family holiday to date. As I gushed about it on the phone to Yvan, a French friend and father of two, he announced, 'Now you are ready for the real thing. But it must be in the South of France. We will wake up, cook some food, have something to drink, perhaps take a walk, drink more wine, and more wine, cook something else, maybe read something and have some wine – and all the while the children are just running and playing outside. I think you will like it.' Me too! And apparently, for the French there is value in having less of some things – though clearly wine is not among them.

Five things to Cut Right Now

1 Birthday party goodie bags

2 50 per cent of:

    – prizes for good behaviour

    – snacks between meals

    – television time for the kids

    – holiday loot

3   The sight of toys in your living room

4   Young child's allowance

5   THE CORD!

Warning Signs

Occasionally, during our little French journey, Oona and Daphne have said or done things that have given me pause long enough to remind myself that this is not France.

Here are a few signals that you may need to temper your new-found Frenchness:

- Your four-year-old has a nightmare that she is lost in Paris and is being hunted by a monster that 'is actually you in a costume'
- Your child develops the habit of reprimanding other kids in the playground and accusing them of being 'very unFrench'!
- You have an extremely hard time hosting play-dates for your children because you cannot tolerate the behaviour of their friends
- You have too many conversations like this:

Daphne: 'Mama, did I do a very good job of not complaining about leaving Celia's house?'

Me: 'Well, you did a normal job. Not complaining is normal. If you had complained, that would have meant you had done a poor job of leaving.'

Daphne: 'Poor?'

Me: 'It would have meant that you did a *not good* job.'

Daphne: 'But I didn't complain. So I did a good job. Complaining is not very French, so I was being French!'

Me: 'Honey, I am not going to congratulate you for just leaving without a fuss. That is now normal for you. And you should always do it and not look for praise.'

Daphne (through tears): 'But I DID do a good job! You should be proud of me!'

7

Les Petits Trésors or Teaching the Art of Living

Not long ago, Mac showed me some home video footage he'd taken of Daphne dancing around the living room – *and on the coffee table*. Initially, my newly installed French-o-meter went berserk at the sight of my child fluttering atop furniture, especially living room furniture! Then the alarm bells in my mind grew fainter as I slowly realized that Daph's dance moves were really quite similar to my own. And I do love a good bop. My pride and delight won over an initial desire to stop the video and have yet another meeting with my girl about boundaries and behaviour. She was so good. (Also, our coffee table is really big and made of strong wood. It does kind of seem like a stage.)

I'm pretty certain that Daphne did not just inherit this style, but rather she developed the steps by watching me during our frequent after-dinner dance parties. I like to think that my signature moves resemble Molly Ringwald's dance in the film *The Breakfast Club*, peppered with a lot of Gothy swoops and a dash of interpretive dance. I'm not sure what the French would make of our regular habit of busting a move before the dishes are even done, but I'm sure they would not approve of a five-year-old bouncing on a table for any reason. So, I split the difference and informed my children that we must always dance if we feel moved to do so, but no one is allowed on the ~~stage~~ coffee table without permission.

The experience of watching Daphne channel me really reinforced how much influence I have on my kids – some of which I'm not even aware of. What could I do with them if I really put my mind to it? What kind of Frenchness, beyond discipline, could I instil? It was all very exciting.

Before setting out on this project, I polled a posse of French parents about that sort of *je ne sais quoi* that they work to imbue in their kids. It did not surprise me that my French connections knew exactly what I was talking about. Three out of nine gave me some version of the following advice: *You only have so long to mould and shape your children. After about age eight or nine, they lose interest in what you teach them. Use your time wisely.*

With Oona, far from babyhood, the clock was ticking especially loud. I asked these parents to list those qualities that they value and endeavour to pass on. These are the ones that came up repeatedly:

- Appreciation of food
- Good citizens/manners

- Good conversationalists
- Sense of style
- *Joie de vivre*
- Appreciation of small, beautiful things
- Good student

I like to think I've already hit the first two (with a rather large hammer), but the other four endowments are certainly worth some effort.

Allons-y!

Good conversationalists

French people often accuse Americans of being boring and Brits of being rude. And we like to protest that they are just uptight snobs. We are not boring and rude – we're fun, but we might not always edit ourselves effectively. And the French are merely well trained (and perhaps a little uptight).

While French children are not encouraged to practise their loquacity in the classroom, French parents are rather intent on raising good conversationalists elsewhere – with real emphasis on the *good*. Even though the French have a reputation for being reserved, I found that they actually do talk a lot; yet for them, conversation is like another art form (think Cyrano de Bergerac).

Once I noticed that very few of my French parent pals would tolerate a dull story from their child, it became exceedingly difficult not to analyze the occasionally lacklustre orations of my own offspring. To me, Oona and Daphne are the two cutest people in the world, so when they launch into a homily on blueberries versus strawberries – for the seventh time – or want me to listen to the plot of their favourite *Phineas and Ferb* episode (again), I don't have much of a problem indulging them. I like to watch their little mouths motor, minds work, and hands gesture. However, this reaction surely isn't the same for everyone – like pretty much every adult that did not give birth to them. Yet, I often see tables of grown-ups halt their conversation when a little person joins their ranks and decides to make a statement – whether or not it has anything to do with the previous adult conversation. It's not uncommon in the States for family meals to be hijacked by the smallest among us, who use the spotlight to make us lift our adult arms up! And then down! And then up again! It's exhausting – and kind of annoying. This would be a definite '*non non*' for a French child.

The French are all about harvesting gracious members of society, so for the parents it is important to teach a child the art of discourse. *Lesson Number 1 – try not to speak unless you have something interesting to say and, if part of a conversation is already in progress, relevant to say.* Of course, French parents aren't going to be harsh on the stories of a three-year-old just mastering language, but I noted that around the ages of five and six, many French kids are urged to step up the level of their chatter (or stop it). I began to acknowledge that even when my girls did not have anything to say, they would just start talking to wrestle their way to centre stage. In their defence, no one had ever told them not to. Whenever they opened their mouths prior to the 'new way', they were generally met with nothing but enthusiasm. I was loath to disparage Oona's and Daphne's little speeches. It seemed like I would, in turn, be criticizing their personalities. Then again, as I became more aware of it, my patience – especially when they interrupted a perfectly enjoyable conversation to offer up something extraneous or mundane – began to wane. I'd seen French mothers chastise their children with a, 'Why are you boring me with this uninteresting story?' and, 'I have already heard about this from you before' – and it sounded so biting. Truthfully, French children are more accustomed to criticism, so I'm sure it did not affect them the way it would the tender pride of my kids. I can only imagine years of future therapy if I said something similar, and so I had to, rather happily, go half-French on this one. I made the case, in a nice, supportive American mom kind of way, that it is important to think about how to captivate your listeners before taking the floor. When a really asinine story hits the airwaves at home, I don't let it go, but I still don't trash it. I might say, 'Tell me something else!' And most importantly, I don't applaud it. Related to this, I've been working on their delivery – particularly the length thereof. If a story is painfully inching along, I let them know. It took a few attempts to explain the phrase 'you're losing your audience' to Daphne, but she gets it now. Both girls are growing more accustomed to developing their thoughts before releasing them out into the world. No one seems scarred, and I don't think I'm just imagining that our dinner conversations have become more intriguing. This little lesson in editing can only help with their charm skills later in life when they are, say, in the school dining area, commanding the attention of a cluster of friends and not their ever-adoring parents.

The other half of this equation, of course, is cultivating a knack for listening. *Lesson Number 2 – learn to listen*. For Daphne this has not been easy. She often reminds me of a humanized R2-D2, the fictional character in *Star Wars*, manically leaning on one foot and then the other, trying not to erupt while waiting to add her legitimate two cents in a conversation. I have a hard time not laughing outright when this happens because it is so pathetically adorable, and as soon as Daph can concentrate on what others are saying and not direct every ounce of her energy towards keeping a lid on things, we'll really be getting somewhere.

Looking ahead, some added savvy in the articulation department will also serve any American or British kid who grows up and attends a party in France, where most likely they will encounter a number of fervent arguments on everything from orange zest to politics. These kinds of conversations are like sport, and there is rarely any ill will imparted.

The first time I witnessed this phenomenon at a French get-together, I consciously backed away from two Frenchmen who were deep in a rollicking exchange about the Gaza flotilla raid, fearing that they were about to get physical and have a punch-up. And then, like nothing had happened, they switched their conversation to the Marseille football club and were next seen raising a glass together. These fellas did not appear offended by each other in the least – to the contrary, they were delighted. I've heard it said that the mark of a good dinner party for the French is when the conversation gets heated and a vocal melee ensues. I am easily inflamed when people have the gall to disagree with me, and these French-style interactions provided a worthy new perspective.

I do pity the clown (often me – yes, I pity myself) who disagrees with Daphne. It doesn't take much for Daph's spikes to come out, so I'm particularly keen on implementing this offshoot to the art of conversation. The French are so very opinionated, and yet they do not seem particularly sensitive – unless, of course, they are in love. I like this. With skin about as thick as paper vellum, Oona and Daphne could use a dose of Frenchness in their metaphorical epidermis. *Lesson Number 3 – let the discourse begin!*

Sense of style

I must admit, my French informants who ranked 'style' high on their lists all had one foot in the States. For instance, two of them have American spouses and visit here often, and one, let's call her Gina, is an American who married a Frenchman. Perhaps these sources are particularly sensitive to the subject of style and presentation because they have seen, first hand, the differences between the States and France. Thinking back to her own, initially rocky, transition to life in France, Gina remembered: 'I had to get used to sprucing myself up even for the playground. No more sweatpants, that's for sure. I hated it at first, but now I guess I'm happy about it. It's good to look good. I go home and sometimes see grown people out in pyjama pants, and it kind of makes me sad.'

There's a reason Jerry Seinfeld once devoted an entire episode of his comedy series to this issue, and declared that his pal George, who had begun wearing sweatpants out of the house, had, in effect, 'given up'. Me – I'm not yet ready to give up.

My guess is that for the native Frenchies, the custom of careful dress is so ingrained in their psyches that they don't even realize how forcefully they pass it on down the line – for them, it would be like listing 'the ability to breathe' as something they hold dearly.

Before going any further, however, I'm going to borrow from my previous sentence and swap in 'style' for 'careful dress'. The French always look tasteful and put-together, but the rebel in me (the one that still owns (and wears) leopard-print creepers – those punk-rockabilly shoes with the enormous soles that are probably less common in a French playground than the sweatpants) does not necessarily equate this with style.

Whatever you want to call it, the French mince no words when it comes to the outfits their children put together. For them, careful dress is a sign of consideration for both the company one keeps and the activities they engage in. According to Susanne, a mother from southern France, whenever visitors come to her home, her two young children are expected to greet them at the door, winsomely dressed and with their hair combed. By the way, she also insists that they look all callers in the eye during the requisite salutations. You'd never see Susanne's children lounging on the sofa in their pyjamas and playing on a Nintendo DS if you arrived for a planned visit. She remarked that this would convey 'that we feel too lazy to have company'. I can see where she's coming from, but I also wanted to counter, 'Ease up, lady!' (But I didn't.)

From what I've seen, French parents, mostly the moms, don't think twice about sending children back to their room to try again if they've selected a poor clothing combo. My friend Peter, who had been brought up just outside Paris, remarked, 'Until she was eighteen years old, my mother would send my sister back to her room to change. Oh, how my sister hated it!' When I naïvely asked what her sister would do, he gave me a look that said, *what do you think?* – 'Of course she went and changed. What else could she do?' I'm still getting used to that.

I do wish I had a similar power, especially for those times when Oona emerges looking like a lunatic who dressed in the dark. Sometimes it seems as though she is going for some kind of *Guinness Book of Records* entry for most number of patterns worn at one time. But again, I suffer from the fear that I'll be corking her bubbling individuality. And then I wonder, was it self-expression that impelled her to select the flowy, pastel-flowered shirt with a Peter Pan collar to go with navy sweatpants, or did she go there because she didn't know any better – or perhaps, because she didn't really care. Either way, it became clear that someone should step in – and *évidemment*, that someone was me. One French mother suggested I number code all of Oona's and Daphne's clothes, as her own mother had done for her: i.e. any 1s can be worn together, any 2s are fair game, and so on. I gave it some thought, but this method, while perhaps a little more gentle than declaring 'You look ridiculous in those clothes. Go and change!' is too neurotic – not to mention time-consuming – for me.

I found my solution by simply bringing up the concept of fashion sense with my kids. In fact, I even turned our little style sessions into a game – very American – called *Dans la Mode*. After Oona and Daphne accepted that this had nothing to do with ice cream, they got into it. Every so often (particularly on a wet day, when going out is not very appealing) we'll take all of their clothes out of the drawers, separate them by species (i.e. leggings in one pile, shirts in another, etc.) – and then lay out the outfits on the bed and *discuss* them together. Kids, by the way, love clipboards – at least mine do. We made a little sheet with categories to think about when reviewing ensembles, including *colours*, *shapes*, *overall feeling*, and *season*. For Daph, who can't read yet, I drew little pictures next to each division. Inevitably, she ends up trying things on and performing a little show. Before you get visions of me being a raging stage mom, I swear it is not like that at all. We still listen to the album *Free to Be . . . You and Me* and I won't force them to wear something they hate – I'm just helping out a little, like a *mère française*.

The hard part is when Daphne materializes wearing an outfit that, while technically matches, still manages to be insane. Picture this: royal blue leggings bespattered with big pink stars and a pink T-shirt, overlaid with a light blue sleeveless leotard featuring flouncy attached tutu. And high red boots with multiple straps and zips to top the look off. And a hair thingy. (OK – I suppose I need to be a little more selective about what I buy for them as well.) She was beaming with pride. I knew that I would have to search pretty far for a French mother who'd allow this get-up (not *at all* dissimilar from something a professional wrestler might sport) out of the house. Well, at least she matched . . .

I almost laughed orange juice out of my nose while having breakfast with Belinda, a mother of three from California who sends her children to a French-American school. As about 50 per cent of the students at the school are French (as in 'from France'), Belinda has had plenty of opportunity to observe the style differences. She told me:

> First of all, you should know that my mother-in-law can barely stand to go out in public with my daughters. They are toddlers, so I don't really mind that they have wild hair and dress like they're constantly on hallucinogens. But this is severely painful to my husband's mother's French sensibilities. It is truly torture for her. I admit, my girls are noticeably more unkempt than the other kids in their pre-school, but this is not a normal school. For instance, one of the parents actually started her own children's clothing label so that

she could have the appropriate French kind of apparel for her son. The clothes are cute, and also utterly ridiculous – like short trousers that stop right above the knee and little caps. That style of trouser-shorts is very French to me. I remember seeing this father at the playground once wearing those shorts with a blue and white striped shirt, like a gondolier would wear, buttoned down to show some chest, a black vest and a beautiful kind of gnarled wood necklace with gold, and then red patent-leather Birkenstocks. I remember thinking, 'He's not gay, just French'.

Side note: I've been racking up quite a few nice little comments from the moms around school who've noticed an improvement in my own look lately (this, by the way, was not hard to accomplish for someone who used to be part of the sweatpants set). In explaining that it was a by-product of our little coup d'état at home, I realized that part of the reason I have the time in the morning to primp a bit is because I am no longer tending to the every whim of my kids. Then again, my oldest friend has become creative and simply puts her son to bed in the clothes (always a tracksuit) that he'll be wearing to school the next morning, thus buying herself more time. Victor Hugo once said that 'The French Revolution was the anointing of humanity.' I'm not sure he meant buying more time in the morning by putting one's kids to sleep in tracksuits but, in any case: Amen, brother!

Joie de vivre

Of course this is a high priority for the French – the phrase is so familiar it needs no translation. I thought it was endearing that the French parents I polled actually mentioned this as something they wanted to foster in their children. I had thought it was one of those phrases that we love to repeat and run with because they are so quaint, but secretly I feared it had little to do with the reality of French life.

Fear not.

This is a kind of 'pay-off' priority. Without well-mannered, self-sufficient, good-conversationalist children who appreciate small beautiful things (for example), the French could never have taken home the championship belt as the nation that spends more time than any other eating, sleeping and shopping (this from a recent study conducted by the OECD, the Organization for Economic Cooperation and Development, an international economic organization of over thirty developed countries). And make no mistake, it's not that the French eat and buy more, but rather they take their time and enjoy themselves. I'm sure that added shopping time is spent on selecting fresh, delightful ingredients for a meal, which will then be lingered over for hours while they engage in lively conversation (uninterrupted by any dull musings from their youngest citizens). It's all part of the lifestyle. As the French also took home the silver for second place in life expectancy, it may not be such a bad one to imitate.

Many French people value time spent with family and happiness over economic prosperity. In a 2010 study, they had the best record for using all of their vacation days (this is saying a lot, as they have the most generous allotment in the developed world). Some 89 per cent of French people took all their holiday allocation, compared with 57 per cent of Americans, who often preferred to be paid in lieu of days off. And how about those fierce riots when President Sarkozy upped the French retirement age to sixty-two?

It's clear that the little Frenchies are watching. A mini riot broke out not long ago among schoolchildren when a false rumour broke out that Sarkozy wanted to eliminate several school holidays. I wonder, was this due to *joie de vivre* or aversion to *l'école*?

On a smaller scale and with fewer burning cars, in my home we have made major strides in discovering the joy in food. In addition to our attempts to revamp our eating rituals on a daily basis, we've now also introduced the 'Saturday Night Spectacular (SNS)' to the mix. (The girls were in charge of the name.) Saturday is now sacred, and nary a play-date or craft lesson will be scheduled after 4 p.m. Or, if we absolutely have to (some things, like the 'Latke Fest' we are going to this Saturday, cannot be missed) cut into this time, we devotedly protect Sunday afternoon and evening for the SNS.

This is how it works: sometime during the week we get together and devise a menu with starter, vegetable course, main course and dessert. Although Daphne has lobbied to permanently be assigned dessert, each week we're all given a different focus. This week, Daphne is on 'hors d'œuvres duty' and she has suggested 'little hot dogs wrapped up in ham'. I might have to work with her on that. So once we know what we are going to make we start gathering, sometimes picking up supplies on the way home from school, but other times getting it all on Saturday. When the time is nigh, we cook everything together – *from scratch* – set the table with the candelabrum and wine glasses for everyone (and no, the girls aren't getting the leaded stuff yet – only juice or soda water in their goblets), and most often end up lounging and laughing around the table for over an hour.

I didn't realize that Oona and Daphne were loving these dinners as much as Mac and me until we were forced to miss one and Oona cried her eyes out. She had wanted to make carrot and ginger soup. Who are these kids?

Meanwhile, my concerted efforts to get them to find the value in extended sleep are a work-in-progress.

Appreciation of small, beautiful things

This French penchant is related to *la joie de vivre*, yet it is its own animal, and thus deserving of some first-class scrutiny. Edith Wharton (the real E.W., not Oona) once described the French as 'a race of artists'. After observing how they pass this reverence for beauty down the line, I now understand why Wharton implicated the entire population in her quote. I also now have more perspective on, sadly, my most vivid memory from high school French class when my teacher, Madame Prideux, stopped in front of each of our desks (more than twenty) with an outstretched hand so that we could admire her rings: 'All ze gems are real. I do not wear fake jewellery. Aren't zay beautiful?' This was an all-girls Catholic school, which makes it a little less weird – but only a little. Even though I barely looked up from drawing on my shoes and thinking Madame Prideux was a snob, I remember clearly that they were emeralds. Now, in retrospect, I feel a little bad. She was just being French and trying to instil a little *taste* in us – a motley crew of California teenagers dripping in accessories from Contempo Casuals. As a French mother, she probably couldn't have helped herself.

Beauty, however, doesn't have to come from swanky jewels for the French to take note. And that's just it, they like to stop and observe, as well as make time to create beauty. I once witnessed a seven-year-old French boy spend at least forty minutes arranging the hors d'œuvres (a more comely array than anything I've ever put together . . .) before the arrival of his grandparents for a weekend visit. Halfway through his task, the little guy asked his mother if they could take a quick trip to the park to collect some stones he'd seen the previous day, speculating that they would look nice next to the radish flowers. Seriously, kid? The request was denied because the park was a good twenty minutes away, but the mom, in turn, sat down and contemplated a number of alternatives to the decorative stones. He finally settled on a few dandelions from their front garden to break up the sea of red.

In my house, for Oona and Daphne, it's all about efficiency. They will race through a colouring book in ten minutes, as though they think that as long as they tag each page with a little bit of colour it is good to go. I've heard the horror stories about French teachers forcing children as young as three to crayon within the lines, using 'appropriate' colours. That's definitely not what I'm after; rather, this particular French lesson is more about taking time. I'm all for colouring faces purple and adding an extra limb here or there to Mickey Mouse and his friends – I'd just like my kids not to be so obsessed with the quantity of what they produce and the speed at which they do this. This goes for handwriting too. Sometimes I hear a little voice within me saying, 'Who cares? Everyone uses computers now, anyway', yet ever since I began striving to get French, another, stronger voice tells me that it is all related to an urgency that charges so many aspects of my children's lives. And I love pretty handwriting. So now one of my most familiar mantras is, 'Slow down, Oona.' It's not exactly George Harrison material, but, hey, I'm busy.

In France, the kids are still taught how to write with fountain pens to avoid the unsightly *pattes de mouche* (little ink trails that resemble fly footprints) which can be caused when using a ballpoint pen. This ain't France.

In a very general way, my girls come by it honestly, as many of us tilt towards efficiency over beauty and literally forget to stop and smell/colour in the roses. But how to counter this inkling in my little French pursuit? I have made Oona work on her handwriting and suggested that Daphne go back and spruce up her colouring, but I'm afraid I simply turned this into another chore for them. I had hoped for them to really feel it – like that imaginary French kid in my mind.

To counter this, the only thing I could think to do was to deliberately seek out to find – and relish in – beauty. I called it 'Sublime Time' in the hope that the girls would be more interested in something with a smart name (go ahead and scoff, but it has worked wonders in the past). I'd announce something like, 'We are going for a walk, and everyone must point out five things they find beautiful and explain why.' Lamentably, early on this also gave birth to another new appellation, 'Daphne's Sublime Time Whine': 'This is boring. Why can't we just go home or to the playground?' Mercifully, like almost everything we've tried, she got used to it. She even got into it. To my delight and, I'll admit, surprise, there was definitely something new going on with the girls the last time we visited the Metropolitan Museum. It's not like Oona and Daphne were opining on the use of shadow in Caravaggio's late works, but they didn't just run through with blinkers on, only stopping momentarily at things that might include a funny cartoon (as in days of yore), asking when we could hit the cafeteria. We spent a lot of time with the Flemish. Too much? Let's just say a lot.

Good student

This priority has given me cause for some extended thought and investigation. It's kind of a toughie, and if ever I was granted the ability to magically blend our two cultural approaches on just one portion of this puzzle, I'd use it on education (or discipline . . . oh, I can't decide . . .). The truth is, the discipline we can revamp on our own, but as the French, American and UK school systems are so vastly different, I would need the assistance of a genie for any transformation. But that doesn't mean we still can't learn a little from our friends in France.

I find the French approach to education fascinating – and also a little terrifying. It's complicated. Because of this, everything – including Daphne's kindergarten parent–teacher meetings – is put through the French sieve, and nothing goes unquestioned. By the time I managed to bring my jawbone back up to its proper position on my face, the aforementioned meeting was almost over. Daphne's teacher had just finished telling us how Daph was one of the most dutiful, willing and obedient pupils in her class. *Really?*

Mac and I were both so surprised that I'm afraid we squandered at least one of our allotted ten meeting minutes in shocked silence trying to imagine our little combustion engine of a child sitting quietly at her desk during lessons. And of course I couldn't help thinking: *how delightfully French.*

The Daphne behaving well part was French – the meeting itself was anything but. I'm told that in France, parent–teacher meetings last about an hour and a half – and there are often cocktails involved. Maybe that is the answer to teacher burnout here in the USA and in the UK. The job might seem less exhausting and thankless with some regular libations. I am only half-kidding here, as I once witnessed the teacher's dining room table at a *collège* (kind of like a middle school) in France set for luncheon with multiple bottles of wine – on a typical, nothing special Thursday, mind you. I read that day's menu as well, and remember thinking that a teaching gig in France might just be the ticket, if only for lunchtime.

Ever since a twelve-year-old Parisian girl beat me in a speed round of listing the country capitals of Europe, I have had a hunch that there is something to be gained from a good look at the way the French school their kids. In my defence, she lives in Europe *and* there's been a lot of redrawing, additions and subtractions to the map I studied in high school. Moldova? (Chişinău, dammit!) Then again, this kid was twelve and would have won even if I'd had all the time in the world.

My friend Paul, an alumnus of French National Education himself, commented that the only way to go to a bad school in France is to pay for it. In other words, French public schools are generally excellent. No shock there, perhaps, as the French Ministry of Education is among the top five largest employers in the world. Because French education is so centralized and organized, unless they are being privately educated, students in all regions of France are taught the exact same curriculum – and for these *étudiants*, school is not fun and games, but honest to goodness work. OK – so although I can't do a whole lot about the American national system of education, I can try to weave in a bit of this French attitude.

When Oona first started school, I worried that the New York City School District mandate for homework in kindergarten would drain her and squelch any enthusiasm for learning. I was so stuck on the idea that, after a string of post-school meltdowns within the first month, Mac and I began touring private institutions. We fell in love with the Waldorf school not too far from us in Brooklyn, but soon realized that this was not an option unless we won the lottery. Instead, I decided that we'd just ignore the homework all together. (In hindsight, maybe it was the constant play-dates and dance classes that had Oona coming unglued every evening.) And so – Oona did not do any of the kindergarten homework. Her American mom said that she didn't have to. For fun (of the masochistic sort), I now like to imagine how that would have gone down in a French school.

Save for their luxurious – and delicious – parent–teacher meetings, French parents don't spend a whole lot of time in the classroom. They're not welcome. In fact, if a parent wants to speak with a teacher, they typically have to make an appointment with the school secretary, often a lengthy process, and they also must have a really good reason. When a child is in school in France, the school is in charge. There's no barrage of emails asking for parent volunteers to come and clean the hamster cage or read during library time. Again, I know this is not a fair comparison and that constant budget cuts have necessitated an even greater classroom presence for American parents. Still, I find the French outlook on school intriguing, and have selectively chosen elements of it to emulate, particularly their habit of making school a top priority in the lives of their children.

For French parents, it is when their kids come home from school that they must really step up. First there is the homework – which is *not* insubstantial. But also, French children are ranked in the classroom, and teachers read their scores aloud on a daily basis. No parent wants their kid to be announced last and used as the example of how not to be (alas, humiliation is also a common practice *à l'école*), so the pressure is really on for parents to make sure their little student understands the lessons on a daily basis. This French priority of raising a good student may be crucial to keeping the kids from being completely dejected.

I'll admit it, I've become obsessed with French education. Throughout the country, schools convene on Monday, Tuesday, Thursday and Friday. The hours of operation are usually 8.30 to 4.30 (give or take fifteen minutes), which explains how they make up for Wednesday (although I'm sure they aren't looking at it that way). I love this. Oh, how I wish the French hours were one of those elements I could incorporate. French children don't expect a whole lot after school because it's already pretty late and they have homework to do. As one mom from Dijon said, 'We just go home, tend to the school work, have a little dinner and then Luc goes to bed.' Luc, her son, is eight. My girls seem to think that their days start once school finishes at 2.50, and when I'm on pick-up duty I usually get hit with a 'What are we going to do today, Mom?'

'I know! How about homework, dinner and bed . . . ?'

These days, Oona rarely has a problem getting her homework done, but until I toughened up I would often let her pound it out over breakfast or even in the car on the way to school. *Désolé*, darling. Homework comes before anything else after school. Ever since I've stopped allowing the girls to watch television on schooldays, this hasn't been too difficult to implement. It's a beautiful thing when priorities collide.

Let's head back to the classroom to feed my infatuation just a little more. It's there you'll find that French teachers aren't big on praising effort, improvement – or even perfection. Just about every lesson is graded out of a possible twenty points. That big twenty is rather elusive, though. One French mom told me that she thought it was illegal for teachers to give a twenty out of twenty. Having grown very accustomed to smiley faces and 'good job!' stamps on everything that comes home, this sounds overly rigorous. On the other hand, I don't want my kids thinking that school is supposed to be fun. It can be, and that's great. But there is also work involved.

In speaking with Americans who have moved their families to France, the primary concern I detected for their ex-pat kids is consistently the French schools. It's not that these transplants worry their children won't get a good education (oh, they will), rather they fear the rigidity of the system. And rightly so. There is not a lot of time spent assessing learning and behavioural disorders in French schools. Anton, a father of two French schoolchildren, recalled:

I laughed when my little daughter came home and said that she wanted to be a road sweeper. I guessed that her teacher had said that if you do not work hard at school, you will be a road sweeper. My teachers would scare us with the same thing when I

was a young student. Maybe this teacher didn't
know it could sound like a fun job to a six-year-old.

Cute story, kind of . . . But I can see why some non-
natives might feel trepidation. Pressure on a
kindergartener? Anton later added: 'They do not look
for things like ADHD and learning disorders here in the
same way as in the United States. To these kids, they say
"do better so you can pass your Bac, or you will be sweeping the streets."' The 'Bac', short for Baccalauréat, is the
greatest weight on young Frenchies. It is a qualifying
exam that most students take after they complete their
secondary education (like high school), and the score
determines where and if they can go on to further studies. In other words, this test determines the rest of their
lives. But no pressure.

Let's take stock. In my perfect, French-American
hybrid world, I would incorporate a little of the inbred
focus and seriousness on education, the genius school
hours and, of course, *les cocktails*. I'll leave behind the
enormous pressure, humiliation, and possible overlook-
ing of kids with special needs.

To reiterate, the French aim to raise expert little racon-
teurs, but the classroom is definitely not the place to
practise their storytelling. The teacher does the talking
and the kids do the listening – unless the teacher calls on
them. I frequently heard from folks with a foot in both
France and the USA that the type of open dialogue
common in the States, with children encouraged to ask
questions and challenge ideas, does not exist in a French

classroom. As one American mom with kids in a French school put it, 'There isn't much emphasis on individual thinking, teamwork, or building self-esteem.' The French teacher knows everything. When I toured schools in France, I noticed that often, especially at *les colleges* and *les écoles secondaires* (middle schools and high schools), the teachers stand on a platform so that they are slightly elevated and, quite literally, looking and talking down to their students.

As strict and hard-edged as this may sound, there is some value to such differences in the teacher–student relationship – the foremost of which is that French students must respect their *professeurs*. At least to their face. In France, it is not the teachers who are degraded and ranked by performance, it is the children. If a student does not study hard enough to pass on to the next level, this will not be considered the fault of the teacher. That child may just become a road sweeper. Actually, for those students who do not perform well on the Bac test, the French government also provides further education in the form of technical schools. Great in theory, except for the fact that this is determined in their teenage years. When Robert Frost wrote 'College is a refuge from hasty judgment', it appears he was not talking about France.

The French are hasty when it comes to learning, and children had better catch on quick, or suffer some of that notorious humiliation. My heart broke when I heard my American friend describe her ten-year-old's trials at school in Paris:

As the French schooling system commonly does . . . they seize any opportunity to use a student's poor performance as an example of what not to do. And that's exactly what happened. Poor Rita. She reported that the teacher repeated, staccato style, '*Vite, vite, vite*!' when she was labouring at the board, and when she wasn't 'getting it' quickly enough, her teacher turned to the class with upturned hands, a shrug of his shoulders, and a roll of his eyes. Then the class laughed at her. She was mortified. Fortunately, we had forewarned the girls, at the beginning of the school year, that their days of the 'nurturing the whole child' mentality were over.

Again, I prefer to leave the humiliation in France.
    'Hey, teacher! Leave them kids alone!'

I took a look at the corresponding curricula for French and American schoolchildren, and on paper they are not so dissimilar, outside of the fact that the French begin the mastery of a foreign language (or two) early on, and on a recent curriculum for French kindergarten they listed 'Civics and Morals', where 'students learn the rules of politeness and social behaviour'. So not surprising.

The real difference is in attitude. Luckily for the American kids, there are such things as second chances.

These top priorities listed by my French confidants are all so sound and significant that it made me wonder why it took studying childrearing in France for me to elevate them. This, in turn, started me thinking about why we are so divergent in the first place.

For example, on the first day of school this year, a few of my friends who opted not to have children were griping about their Facebook feeds being inundated with back-to-school photos. Due diligence had me immediately wondering how this played out in France. Turns out French parents generally do not post as much about the adorable and daffy shenanigans of their kids. This is due, probably, to a combination of factors: the French are more private to begin with; they tend to keep their family lives separate from their social lives; and – the clincher – they are not so consumed with the lives of their offspring.

So it goes.

I just logged on to Facebook for an honest assessment, and there is obviously some truth in what my kids have been repeating of late – I am not French. We are not French. My wall is awash in photos and videos of Oona and Daphne, and little else. Mac is more diverse than me with his postings, but I wouldn't really say that he's gone French here either, especially as he has a Twitter feed devoted to the whimsy that often springs forth from Oona and Daphne. We can't seem to help ourselves. But I don't want him to. If Mac had gone full French, he never would have Tweeted these gems, among many others:

Oona, finishing her waffle: 'Can I lick my plate?' Me: 'Sure.' So she did and said: 'Great, and barely any syrup in my hair, too.'

Daphne: 'I don't want to be bad, so I'm gonna stop being bad . . . until Christmas.'

Me, watching a group of teenagers walk past us: 'Are you excited at the thought of being a teenager some day?' Oona: 'Like – no!'

Daphne: 'Why do I have to brush my teeth?' Me, exhausted: 'Because everyone brushes their teeth.' Daphne: 'Robots don't.' Me: 'OK, good point.'

Oona, apparently having been successfully marketed to: 'Does my hair look 100 per cent shinier?'

Catherine left Daph's bed for Oona's last night: 'I'd rather stay here for a bit.' Oona: 'Sure, I seem to have lost my sense of squirm.'

Oona, making a pretty airtight case: 'We weren't fighting; we just had different thoughts.'

Daphne, to me: 'You farted. It sounded like, "Leave me alone!"'

'Am I good at interrupting?'

Me, watching Daphne give my breakfast cereal a deep-tissue massage: 'Please don't touch my cereal.' Daphne: 'I'm not.'

Then again, if we were more efficacious in the good French fight, my kids wouldn't have said 90 per cent of the above. But they did, and I'm not French. I'm just doing my best to uncover the useful bits of their child-rearing ways – and along the road I'm reminded of all the things I love about my homeland, particularly our big, messy humour and pluck. To borrow a turn of phrase from Royal Tenenbaum, another of my cinematic flames, we've got a lot of 'grit, fire, and guts' going on in this country.

So, how is it that we ended up so different from the French, anyway? No one can deny that our relationship with them is *un peu* fraught because of these disparities. For many, it's a love–hate type of situation. Kind of like the little boy and girl in the playground who spend all of their time pestering each other and claiming to loathe each other, but nestled down in there amid the conflict there's also fascination, and a bit of a crush.

I turned to journalists Jean-Benoit Nadeau and Julie Barlow and their book *Sixty Million Frenchmen Can't Be Wrong (Why We Love France But Not the French)* to try to get a better understanding of why this is. Nadeau and Barlow spent two years in France on a mission to really define for us non-natives what makes the French so very . . . French. The authors point out in the very beginning that much of this clash stems from the fact that we judge them against our own standards, even though

different things move the French – as if they had different ropes, gears, and springs inside them.

Oddly, Anglo-Americans can see that the Japanese, the Chinese, and the Indians are different, and that these fundamental differences shape national characters and the way things are done in those societies. Why can't we do this with the French?

Although I scrutinized the French in a dire attempt to get a grip on my wayward parenting practices, I've found it helpful to keep Nadeau and Barlow's observation in mind; we are very different cultures coming from very different perspectives. There needn't be a winner here (and yet there's no reason not to poach a few French practices that can bring a little tranquillity to my home).

The most common stereotype inflicted on the French that comes to my mind is that of pomposity. The words 'French' and 'snob' are almost as linked as 'Nutella' and 'baguette'. (Wait – am I the only one who links those two words so often?) Now that I've dipped deeper in, rather than 'snobby' I would describe the French as 'particular' (apologies again, Madame Prideux). And this makes sense if considered in an historical context. Whereas Americans are very comfortable trying out new things – we are a nation of frontiers people, after all – it's not so natural for the average French citizen, who's been living in a country that's steeped in traditions, many of which haven't changed for centuries. Nadeau and Barlow point out that

The ancestors of the French go back several ice ages. They are not a people who, like North

Americans, arrived in the midst of a primitive
culture, erased it, and started over. They have
always been there. There was plenty of upheaval
throughout French history, but no definitive break
with the past . . . [and when we] are faced with
France's peculiar way of doing things, [we] do not
reason that [we] are dealing with an ancient people
who have their own way of doing things.

When it comes to doing things like making their kids
obey, I'm all ears.

And a little perspective is always a good thing, as well.
Take, for instance, the French approach to money, which
is very different from our own. Whenever I'm in France I
marvel at those big, beautiful shutters on the multitudes
of old buildings. I find them very romantic, yet I always
wondered why they are so huge. It wasn't until I read
Nadeau and Barlow's theory about the old system of
taxation in France that I saw how these charming facets
of old French architecture have a much deeper purpose
than making me lightheaded, or even keeping out the
sun. Hundreds of years ago, taxes were assessed based on
'apparent' wealth. Tax spies, working for the despised
'tax farmers' (*fermiers généraux*), would look in the
windows to do the assessing, leading to the theory that
these enormous shutters functioned, at least in part, to
block out prying eyes. The heads of more than a few of
these *fermiers généraux* were lopped off during the Revolution, but they still managed to leave a long-lasting mark
on the French psyche. Indeed, this has informed how the

French relate to money, and they are still less likely to make it obvious who has it and who doesn't. This probably has something to do with why they are generally more private than we are.

I learned about this cultural difference the hard way at the end of a wonderful lunch in Paris. A friend of mine had gathered together a few of her colleagues for me to question. The food was, of course, lovely and the conversation was so interesting that I lost track of time. It had been my intention to pick up the tab as a gesture of thanks, but I ended up having to rush out to get to another meeting across town before the bill arrived. So, I did what any American would do, and I left a wad of cash on the table, instructing my friend to please pay on my behalf. Not good. It was as if a record had scratched on the giant turntable of life. And then silence at the table. Thankfully, many of my lunch companions don't speak English and my friend was able to tell me, as *sotto voce* as possible: 'Put your money away. Money is taboo here. You can't do that.' If you've ever wondered how you, too, could feel like an international *imbécile*, this is the way. After I left, those ladies must have found some discreet, classy way to divvy up the bill, but it's still a mystery to me.

And what about the staunch French defence of their language, which is also responsible for some 'snob' slinging? I have been made by French waiters to repeat the word (words?) *l'eau* over and over and *l'eauver* again in an attempt to get a glass of water. Many tourists think this is just an overt attempt by *le garçon* to make us look stupid – and stay thirsty. However, there are some roots to this insistence on the correct pronunciation (even though that server knows exactly what you are talking about). The French are very serious about their French. In 1635 they established L'Academie Française, an organization dedicated to the conservation of the French language and which rigorously oversees any changes to the French dictionary. This might not seem so significant until you realize the kind of power they have. For instance, the French subsidiary of an American company was once slapped with a $650,000 penalty for only proffering software in English (and not French) to its employees. They are not messing around.

I discovered that even the French affection for really cute children's clothes has a fascinating historical explanation. Trawling around on a website devoted to historical boys clothing (yes, this exists: histclo.tripod.com), I came across the term *garçons modèles*, a phrase used to describe little boys who are both impeccably behaved *and* impeccably dressed. The French have a term for this, yet they do not have a word for 'parenting'. That says a lot. Anyway, it is theorized that the aftermath of the Second World War profoundly affected the way French children were dressed. Although there had always been high standards for appearance before the war, children's outfits were more likely to resemble shrunken versions of the prevailing adult costume of the era. Yet, because so many French men died during the war, women started making more decisions – and they took up a children's crusade of sorts. Cool things happened – like child labour being outlawed. Another boon was that kids were treated more like kids in areas such as education, character and . . . dress. And now, one of my favourite things in the world is getting a bag of hand-me-downs from my French friend with a nine-year-old daughter. French kids clothes are *so* adorable and beautiful and whimsical. I am clearly not the only American who feels this way either, as evidenced by the rage for the Petit Bateau line of clothes in the States.

And there is Mac, who after seeing the film *The City of Lost Children*, was obsessively searching for a grey cable-knit sweater with little brass buttons. We seriously scanned vintage and thrift stores for weeks. Actually, Mac might be a special case.

Of course, there are aspects of the French character that I won't be trying to turn out in my family. One of my French pals here in New York says that it can be excruciating when her parents come to the States for a visit and criticize everything. While they do this in France, they usually tend to wait until people (with the exception of their family members) are out of earshot. Here in the USA, they are under the impression that no one speaks French, so they often loudly and freely lambast innocent (and often bilingual) by-standers. Awkward. And unkind.

For my little 'Frenchensteins', we are going to accentu-ate the positive − and the observant, respectful and obedient.

Masculin/Féminin

At about age three, Daphne went through her 'sporty' phase. At the very least, four times each week she insisted on wearing an Ireland soccer jersey with matching nylon shorts that a friend had brought back from a trip abroad. Oona had a similar tomboy chapter, and it was just last summer that she had a hell of a time figuring out what kind of swimsuit to wear. She wanted to go with boys' swimming trunks, but I wasn't (still not, for that matter) quite unconventional enough to allow her to go without a shirt, regardless of how far away from puberty she might be. During both of these identity enterprises, I congratulated myself on providing the kind of atmosphere wherein my kids can comfortably examine their sense of self and experiment with their individuality. (Hello the album *Free to Be . . . You and Me*, again. I do love you.) I'm still into that, but I fear that sometimes parents might go a bit overboard with keeping all options open, and to do so we end up burying our own sexual identities when the children are present. I love the way French parents can be so affectionate with each other and not worry about *the kids*. '*Cette femme a un corps absolument magnifique*' ('This woman has an absolutely magnificent body') – a choice phrase I overheard one happy French dad declare, almost absent-mindedly, in front of his six-year-old *fille*. In my environs, I'm pretty sure such an exposition would likely be seen as damaging to the mind of any young, impressionable daughter. 'Not in front of *the kids*!' But I rather like these celebrations of sexuality. Unfortunately, it has been reported that many a French *père* has the abominable habit of directing similar adoration towards women he's not married to – not at all what I am after.

The French have a long, stalwart tradition of feminism, but their brand is not mutually exclusive to femininity. This is something I'd like to impart to my two girls, whichever style of swimsuit they eventually find the most comfortable. Hopefully they won't chafe, and I'm convinced it will cause less confusion. Also, the occasional French kiss keeps their father and me merry; as they say, a happy mom is a happy kid.

Progress Report, à la French Supernanny

When I first discovered that France had its own Supernanny, I was slightly confused. Why would the French need a hero nanny to swoop in and rescue hapless, hopeless parents from their unmanageable offspring – it's not a French problem, right? I've since learned that not all French children are little angels, and that the entertainment value of the show, in any language, is sensational. There are Supernannies on television everywhere from Sweden to Israel to Brazil. Even China, Tiger-Mother territory, now has a Supernanny (and I shudder at that thought).

Of course, my eyes are locked on France and their

beloved Cathy Sarrai, who catechized, in her blue-suited, bespeckled dictatorial way, how to claim one's inner Chief, until her death in 2010.

But Cathy left behind a trove of French-flavoured advice in my new favourite book, *Super Nanny: tous les bons conseils de Cathy*. At the end of her manual, Cathy provides a little quiz to assess *le progress*. It's long, so here is a condensed version. To be French, you don't want to answer yes to any of Cathy's negatives (−), but to be humane you may want to reconsider her approach to numbers 4 and 9.

Shall we?

1 **Dorment-ils sans problème dans leur lit, sans chercher à venir dans le vôtre? +**
Do they sleep soundly in their beds, without trying to come to yours? +

2 **Leur faites-vous un menu à part? −**
Do you make them a separate menu at meal times? −

3 **Si votre enfant refuse de manger ce que vous avez préparé, lui préparez-vous autre chose? −**
If your child refuses to eat what you have prepared, do you fix him something else? −

4 **Vous parlent-ils comme à un copain? −**
Do they speak to you as though you are a friend? −

5 **Savez-vous rester zen lorsqu'ils font un caprice? +**
Can you remain Zen while they are having a tantrum? +

6 **Savez-vous couper court aux négociations? +**
Do you know how to cut short negotiations? +

7 **Vivez-vous dans l'angoisse constant de l'accident domestique? –**
Are you constantly in fear of a domestic accident? –

8 **Ont-ils une télévision ou un ordinateur dans leur chamber? –**
Do they have a television or computer in their room? –

9 **En cas de problèmes à l'école, donnez-vous a priori raison à votre enfant? –**
In the event of a problem at school, do you take your child's side? –

10 **Vos enfant vous apportent-ils de grands moments de joie? ++++**
Do your children bring you oodles of joy? ++++

8

La Conclusion

When I was just a little older than Oona, I was out selling
'World's Finest Chocolate' bars in my leafy, northern California neighbourhood to raise money for my Catholic
school. (Those bars, by the way, were definitely not the
world's finest.) Actually, I was selling the chocolate to win
a prize, and the proceeds just happened to go to St Charles.
I was determined to earn at least the cocker spaniel stuffed
animal awarded for the third highest seller.

A middle-aged woman came to the door of a house
around the corner from my own. I gave my pitch and she
seemed delighted, but in the end admitted that she would
not be able to buy from me because she was sure the kids
across the street, who also went to my school and whose
parents were good friends with this neighbour, would
most certainly come around with the same proposition,
and they'd be terribly disappointed if she purchased the
chocolate from another seller. I remember thinking, 'Ha!

I know those lazy kids and they are probably playing Atari and stuffing handfuls of Frosted Flakes in their mouths right this second. I *need* this sale! I *want* that dog!' I guess my face didn't betray these feelings, and I must have even smiled because the next day, while I was at school, that lady walked over to my house to tell my mom what a polite and gracious child she had in me – and she left me $1. Not enough for that stuffed spaniel I was not destined to win, but it was something. When my mom recounted it all to my dad, they both visibly inflated into self-satisfied human peacocks.

It used to annoy me when my parents would puff up any time a stranger complimented our good behaviour. 'It's not like *they* did anything,' I'd think. Oh, how wrong I was. As I have learned, they must have done quite a bit to turn out mannered citizens – especially ones that did not even realize their civilities. Somehow, between the time when I was a kid and when I started having kids, I lost sight of how they did it.

The rest is French history, of a sort. By now, you know all about that.

When I picked Oona and Daphne up from a sleepover recently, and the parents began gushing about them – 'Your daughters actually asked if they could be excused from dinner. We will have them over any time you want; maybe they will influence Luke and Isabella. Oh, and Oona apologized for not eating my rice pilaf. Your kids have amazing manners. I wish they would rub off on mine' – I could feel my pride swelling. Well, until I looked over at Oona, whose eyes were rolling at full speed. At that moment, I knew just how my parents had felt, and yet I also understood what Oona was suffering. I remembered how a French friend had once commented on the frequency with which we Americans compliment our children's behaviour, even though it is very often hideous. She postulated that in France, decorum is expected and not always – in fact, it is rarely – congratulated.

Evidently, the real trick is going to be maintaining a healthy balance between French and American parenting techniques. Mac and I have successfully managed to halt the evolution of insolence in our daughters – most of the time – and have even reversed some very obnoxious habits they (and we) had fallen into. But sometimes I worry that I might take it too far and lose perspective in my attempts to be more like that little French parent I can feel sitting on my shoulder barking orders like a lunatic angel. I knew things were getting out of hand while watching *Mary Poppins* with Daphne the other day, I found myself thinking that Poppins was sorely unFrench. I actually began rooting for the authority of George Banks over Mary's more innovative caregiving style. When Mary Poppins isn't safe, it's time for a little self-reflection.

I have to remind myself that the French way is not always without complication and, thankfully, I have a number of memories in the arsenal to help me keep things sagacious. I often find myself thinking back on one night in particular in Los Angeles, when Oona unexpectedly schooled a French father.

Perhaps the worst nightmare for a French parent is being formally questioned about how they created such a well-behaved child and then that child having a melt-down in the middle of a conversation about such good manners. This is exactly what happened when I met with a lovely couple from Normandy, Christian and Annette, and their three-year-old daughter, Celine. Our rendez-vous took place at a friend's rooftop pool. Although we were scheduled to talk in the early evening, Annette was detained at work and we didn't get together until nearly 8 p.m. For a while, Celine was unbelievably complaisant, arriving at the pool after my own kids were already splashing about. Neither of mine will ever threaten Mark Spitz's swimming records. And yet, they were so proud of their achievements (in Daphne's case, this entailed not much more than jumping in by herself wear-ing water wings) that all the adults on the sidelines were unceasingly called upon to watch their dazzling feats: 'Mommy, watch what I can do!' 'Did you see it? I'll do it again!' 'Wait, watch!! I'll show you something really cool.' 'Can you take a photo of me doing this trick?' 'Dad! Uncle Aaron! WATCH!'

So, into the cacophony of loudly solicited praise, little Celine shows up and slips right into the water without comment – or water wings. She proceeds to swim the length of the pool while her parents swiftly join the grown-ups with a bottle of wine. I was so impressed with the new little swimmer that I couldn't help but effuse about her aquatic talent. The kid just looked at me with slight confu-sion and smiled shyly. That is to say, she was French.

After swimming circles around my girls with barely a peep for nearly an hour, Celine had had enough and retreated to her father's lap. Not long after, my own kids followed suit and joined the adults. What happened next I'm not really sure because I was deep in conversation with Annette, but Celine began to howl. After many attempts, her parents were still completely unable to calm her. I thought she had hurt herself, but her father assured everyone that she was fine. Eventually, Annette had to take Celine indoors. After they left the scene, Christian looked at Oona and asked, 'What? Did I do something to her?' Why Christian had turned to a seven-year-old for counsel, I'll never understand. But apparently he went to the right place. Immediately, Oona broke the situation down as she saw it: 'I think that there are a few things bothering Celine. First of all, she is very little and it is late. I think she must be tired. Also, I am not sure that she ate dinner yet. I think she might have been crying about dinner. But actually, what probably made her really the most upset was when you embarrassed her. She was sad about that. I could tell. I wouldn't have liked that very much, either.'

Poor guy. But he did ask.

I wasn't sure whether to be horrified or pleased with my burgeoning psychiatrist. Although gently administered, Oona was publicly dressing down this adult, one she hardly knew, for the way in which he had treated his child. This couldn't possibly be very French, but then again he had asked Oona's opinion. I couldn't help but feel pride for Oona's outspoken interpretation of the situation. Even Christian, now clearly embarrassed himself, seemed impressed by her explanation.

While working on this book I have come up against this strange dynamic with my subjects. Almost everyone I interviewed and observed has been a parent, most often with children in tow. I realized early on how impossible it is not to be self-conscious when you know someone is scrutinizing your kids and how you interact with them. For Frenchies like Christian and Annette, the pressure was on, and for my dear American friends, the defences were up. I am glad to have made it to the other side relatively unscathed. I hope those who participated will agree.

There were, of course, a few casualties during the experiment. Like when I told Daphne that if she didn't shape up, I would get French and cancel a highly anticipated play-date with her bestest pal of the week. Sadly, she didn't heed my warning, so I was forced to call off the fun, via an email to her friend's mom. This might have gone down without a hitch in France, but here in Brooklyn I received a somewhat chafed reply, in which the other mother explained how 'unfair' it was that her child, who was 'devastated' not to have Daphne over, should be punished for Daphne's behaviour. She asked if perhaps I could have 'chosen a more appropriate consequence'. Give me a break. The truth is, however, I haven't used that threat since.

That was early on, though, and these days I rarely even need to heighten the stakes. Even Daph's letter to Santa this Christmas shows evidence of what is going on in her darling little head. She wrote:

Dear Santa,

All of us in America are sorry for our bad behavior, but I'm the sorriest. Speaking of, I want Julie's bunny.

Love,
Daphne

OK, so she's still very much an American kid. And I love her and her American-ness. And Oona too – who I might never convince to slow down and refine her motor skills. I won't stop trying. However, there are times when I wonder if some form of the same principle that applies when a person loses one of their senses, and the other four kick in stronger, might be in play with Oona's sensibilities. When we were out at Fire Island (you may remember those blissful summer days from Chapter 6), she noted that a couple of kids had set up a station near the ferry dock and were selling handmade friendship bracelets to newcomers. Oona cannot resist a commercial opportunity – or a competitive challenge – but she also has little to zero interest (or know-how) in weaving a bunch of bracelets. After thinking it over for half a day, she came up with her own product – 'Poem in a Shell'. She spent the other half of the day gathering shells from the beach and making signs, and by the time the first ferry pulled in the next morning, she was out hawking her wares. She would lure customers in with her charm (and cute little sister) and then propose that, for $1.75, they could give her one word, and she would – on the spot – compose a short poem and then have her father (whose penmanship, lamentably, is not much of an improvement over Oona's) transcribe it with a Sharpie inside the shell. Even the price point, $1.75, was brilliant as nearly every one of her clients gave her $2 and told her to keep the change. In under an hour, she had pulled in $18.

We are going to be just fine.

Maybe even better than fine with a combination of our native instincts ($1.75) and *un peu* more Frenchification. Mac and I are currently cooking up a scheme to live in Paris for a year. *Joie de vivre*, and handwriting, and croissants! I think I may be ready. The other night when we were out to dinner – *sans* kids – we found ourselves talking to a young couple at the table next to us. Eventually, Oona and Daphne came up in the conversation. I almost knocked over our table with happy laughter when the woman said, 'Don't take this the wrong way, but you just don't seem like a mom to me.' Oh, how *delightfully French* I felt.

And not negligent. Or guilty.

To be honest, I did discover that French mothers do experience some guilt. In discussing my findings with Camille, a thirty-two-year-old mother of a toddler named Rose, I asked if she ever wished she could be a stay-at-home mom: 'Sometimes I think that would be nice, but I would never not work – at least while my own mother is still alive. I would feel too guilty and I know she would not approve. Our mothers worked very hard so that we, their daughters, could be in the workforce along with the men. I could not do that to her.'

There are those who will try to argue that French children might be well behaved but, in a sort of quid pro quo situation, they turn into antipathetic older French people. To that I say 'baloney!' or '*balivernes!*' French parents, for the most part, are certainly much more strict, but they are able to be that way while simultaneously flourishing an undeniable closeness with their children. One of the greatest benefits I saw to this method is that after putting in the early work, the French relax more around their kids – not just because their offspring aren't acting like jackasses but because they believe that there is little they can do after a child reaches a certain age. While we struggle to reign in our kids when they hit the tweens, French children are given more freedom. I'm told this leads to less family drama – but I suppose that's the next book.

There will always be a jillion different ideas about parenting, and there is doubtless more than one valuable method out there. I went French in response to an unhealthy dynamic that had taken hold of my home life. The main thing I take away from all of this Frenchy stuff – besides becoming a real scarf wearer – is a hybrid approach that has led to order in the house yet still allows us all to be ourselves. I'll never do things exactly as they are done in the land of Victor Hugo and *escargot*, but I don't need to. For one thing, I can't stand the taste of snails. No matter how much butter and garlic is involved.

This past Thanksgiving, feeling too daunted by the thought of hosting yet again, Mac and I decided to play the restaurant card, as many Americans do. After just over a year of attempting to Frenchify, I experienced, in two and a half hours, the perfect distillation of our achievement. *Two and a half hours*. That's how long Oona and Daphne were able to sit, civilly at the French bistro (where else?) we had chosen for Thanksgiving dinner. They even did a little tsk-ing themselves, as most of the other kids in the joint, fidgety and impatient with the lengthy feast, ran around and flagrantly fussed. It wasn't as though our kids didn't require attention – and a little equipage – to keep it together. We did many *Mad Libs* with Oona at the table, and Daphne kept herself busy building a small cardboard castle with numbered mosaic stickers I had stashed in my purse for her. But we also had great conversations, Martinis (Mac and I), compliments from the serving staff on manners (Oona and Daphne), and a long, luxurious meal. Bon appétit, indeed.

After dinner, we wandered through Korea Town on our way back to the F train bound for Brooklyn. In one sprawling store, we all browsed aisle after aisle packed with books, CDs, DVDs, lipsticks, touristy tchotchkes, and small porcelain figurines of princesses and elves. I braced myself for a full-on, Mach 3 attack of the gimmies, but it never came. Oona asked once about the chances of us buying one of the elf figures, but when we saw it was close to fifty bucks, she stopped asking (bless her penny-pinching heart). Daphne quietly inspected the goods. Let me say that one more time: Daphne quietly shopped. Daphne. *You've come a long way, bébé.*

Acknowledgments

Special thanks goes out to Savannah Ashour, Lise Schreier, Josh Schreier, Jessica Lee Rami, Liana Fructman, Deirdre Veillon, Heather Chaplin, Joanna Ebenstein, Nancy Dillion, Naomi Scott, Aaron Ruby, Dawn O'Leary, Oliver Burkeman, Matt Haber, Jeremy Kasten, Richard Faulk, Caroline Trujillo, Lisa Degliantoni, Linda Phillips, French people everywhere, Google Translate, John Cook, Jenni and Jofie Ferrari-Adler, April Peveteaux, Haleh Stahl, Vickey Finney, Karl Monge, Matt Murphy, Proteus Gowanus, Barbara, Michele, Lance and Pedro, my parents and all of my magnifique siblings and their standout spouses – especially Margie, Billy, Pinn, and Patsy – Eleanor Birne, Joanne Gledhill, Caspian, Arabella and Felicity at Abner Stein, Janis Donnaud and Marnie Cochran, everyone who tended to Oona and Daphne while I was in France (Blanchflower, Eli and Kelly, Ginny), Oona and Daphne, and – most forcefully – thanks to Mac Montandon.

From Byron, Austen and Darwin

to some of the most acclaimed and original contemporary writing, John Murray takes pride in bringing you powerful, prizewinning, absorbing and provocative books that will entertain you today and become the classics of tomorrow.

We put a lot of time and passion into what we publish and how we publish it, and we'd like to hear what you think.

Be part of John Murray – share your views with us at:

www.johnmurray.co.uk

 johnmurraybooks

 @johnmurrays

 johnmurraybooks